ANSWERS BEHIND THE

RED DOOR

Battling the Homeless Epidemic

By Michele Steeb
with David M. Flanagan

Answers Behind the
RED DOOR

Battling the Homeless Epidemic

Plano, Texas
First Edition
Michelesteeb.com

S-CLUB PUBLISHING
1631 Alhambra Blvd. — Suite 120
Sacramento, California 95816

PRINTED IN THE UNITED STATES OF AMERICA

ISBN: 978-1-7360016-9-1

Praise for *Answers Behind the RED DOOR*

"In pre-pandemic and now Covid America, lawmakers seemingly are incapable of addressing a homelessness crisis that embodied shattered lives, afflicted cities and decades of failed government intent. Answers Behind The Red Door provides precisely that – answers and a clear guideline for addressing this most chronic of America's societal woes."

Bill Whalen
Research Fellow/Virginia Hobbs Carpenter Fellow in Journalism
Hoover Institution

"...Michele offers a wealth of information which serves to enlighten and inspire a greater understanding of how lives are saved and forever changed. She brings valuable hands-on experience and a strong sense of responsibility to her work and is truly passionate about helping others successfully overcome the challenges which so often contribute to homelessness. Her expertise and experience, along with her unique perspective and involvement in public policy related to homelessness, shed light and offer sage guidance for decision makers and communities working to address the very serious and challenging issues of homelessness and poverty throughout our nation. Her message is one of hope for a better and brighter future for those in need of help."

Don Nottoli
County Supervisor
Sacramento, CA

"In her nearly 13 years as CEO of *Saint John's*, Michele developed an understanding that (for the homeless) providing a bed was not nearly enough. She made the comparison between her homeless residents and women involved in the criminal justice system, seeing that both populations merged from the same causes: childhood trauma, lack of education, lack of employment, physical and mental abuse and substance abuse disorders. Under her tenure, *Saint John's* built an integrated health unit to assimilate these services to effectively address the root causes of a woman's homelessness… then replicated it for women transitioning from prison. She worked vehemently at the state and national levels to help policymakers understand that for success, a bed plus trauma-informed services is key. *Answers Behind the Red Door* is an example of her continued steadfastness and passion for pursuing what is necessary to heal and invigorate the homeless and incarcerated populations."

Dawn Davison

Retired Warden, Correctional Consultant

"As a former drug dealer who served nearly ten years in federal prison, I accidentally discovered a passion for cooking while incarcerated. Upon release, I was fortunate enough to land as a dishwasher at *Gadsbys* in Beverly Hills, worked my way up to line cook, and eventually becoming the Executive Chef at *Café Bellago.* Along the way, I discovered another deep-rooted passion as well; in helping other incarcerated individuals uncover—that everyone has innate gifts, but so many have grown up in situations that limit their ability to discover it.

Michele Steeb's *Answers Behind the Red Door* addresses homelessness as an epidemic, and one that can actually be cured. It's about helping to unleash people bound by poverty, addiction, violence, and a lack of education so that they, too, can become free to change. In that, we both believe everyone can change and should have the opportunity to live their dream.

Chef Jeff

Award-winning chef, New York bestselling author, public speaker and former Food Network star.

"In her new book, *Answers Behind the Red Door*, Michele Steeb combines compassion with intelligence, and outlines a path for reforming our broken system. She understands both the human challenge of homelessness and the dysfunction of our public policies. *Answers Behind the Red Door* sheds new light on the crisis, which has overtaken West Coast cities—and threatens to undermine the American Dream."

Christopher Rufo
Director of Discovery Institute's Center on Wealth & Poverty

"*Answers Behind the Red Door*—Michele Steeb began a labor of love that included not only shelter and respite to often traumatized women and their children, but programs for job training, case management, addiction recovery, financial literacy and personal relationship competency. She engaged and challenged houses of faith, business leaders, and governmental authorities to join in the work. That engagement eventually became less and less of an 'ask' as *Saint John's Program for Real Change* became an amazing place of true transformation. In short, previously homeless women began to believe in themselves. I have often said that Michele believed in them first before they even could.

...I trust Michele as she allows us a peek behind the *Red Door* to understand the institutional challenges these women and children (and the organizations that seek to walk with them) have to navigate in our country. She will never be silent because she so firmly believes we can all be and do better. And if Michele starts believing that for us, I trust we will all eventually find that we believe it ourselves. There are few people one gets to know in life that really catches your attention, not just because they're big-hearted, but because they help others to grow...in both their worldview and in their life mission, too."

Pastor Frank Espegren
St. John's Lutheran Church, Sacramento

Because there so much data included in this book, and because we wanted to make it as easy as possible on the reader, the decision was made to incorporate all data sources within the book narrative itself, as opposed to the use of footnotes or a typical bibliography. If additional information or questions arise, your requests are appreciated and welcomed.

– *michelesteeb.com.*

TABLE OF CONTENTS

While this book focuses on the homelessness crisis in America, in a sense, it really isn't about that at all. At the very heart of this book is a message regarding the need to address the hidden, misunderstood, underlying issues that often lead people into homelessness in the first place.

Mental Illness and Addiction (considered to be a form of mental illness) are conditions defined by both the National Institute of Health (NIH) and the Center for Disease Control (CDC). These diseases, in addition to experienced trauma, are most often at the very root of an individual's homelessness in upwards of 75% of the cases (national research cited later). Left unaddressed, adults continue to grow more and more sick; and the children...are more likely to become homeless as adults.

For this reason, Priscilla Cochran-Navarra was asked to write the Foreword. The very nature of her work at Child Protective Services (CPS), indeed the nature of CPS' work on the whole, is to address the causal issues which prevent people from reaching their full potential.

"Butterflies cannot see their wings. But the rest of the world can."

Foreword

BY PRISCILLA COCHRAN-NAVARRA

When I first started my career with Sacramento County Child Protective Services (CPS) ten years ago, I had no idea what to expect. I knew CPS existed but was clueless about the inner workings of this county agency. That would change, and very quickly.

My official title is Family Service Worker. I supervise and/or observe court ordered visitations between children that have been removed from the home and their parent(s) while the case is being investigated. In the most severe cases, I have gone to hospitals and sat with children injured by someone who was supposed to protect them. Reasons for a child's removal include drug/alcohol abuse (80-90% of my caseload), neglect, domestic violence, and sexual abuse.

Every time I feel that I have "have seen it all," I witness something even more horrific than the time before. My many tears could fill a river, but the moments of doubt and sorrow have been far overshadowed by the moments I could bring comfort to a hurting child during the most tumultuous time in his or her life.

The immediate effects of this trauma on the children are often clear. For example, a child who is victim to violence in the home often emulates those actions in times of frustration and anger—acting out by biting, kicking, yelling, and hitting is quite common behavior. I have seen teens engaging in risky sexual activity, including prostitution, often introduced to these behaviors by a parent. I've even witnessed daughters and sons "pimped out" by a drug addicted parent in order to fund the next fix.

Data indicate the long-term effects of childhood trauma result in high-risk behaviors such as unprotected sex and substance abuse—my caseload is living proof. They also illustrate links to chronic illnesses such as depression, heart disease, and cancer.

I have seen some of these children heal, in spite of their physical and mental wounds, if they receive services to address and heal from the trauma experienced AND if their parent(s) develop the tools to lead a very different life.

Depending on the case, CPS may require parents to take classes in parenting, domestic violence, and substance use disorder (SUD), to engage in individual and/or family therapy, to appear for the visits with their children, and to remain sober. By requiring these services, especially sobriety, the hope is that parents will learn a different way.

Our system must do both: provide parents with the tools to change while helping them, and their children, heal from the trauma they experienced in order to end the cycle permanently. In my ten years with CPS, I have never known a parent to show up willingly on our doorstep. Without the requirements imposed on them, including the removal of their children and the requisites to reunification, nothing changes.

I believe in *Saint John's* model for these reasons—the incredible services they provide to parents and their children, and the requirements that parents engage in those services to ensure the best chance of success for the families they serve.

Over the past decade, I have remained in contact with several children who received these services and whose parents did as well. I noticed a difference right away. Children once beaten, battered, neglected, and broken, now hold their heads high with smiles on their faces. Through the onslaught of adversity, these children have risen from the ashes. I am so incredibly proud to have been a part of their story, and so incredibly proud to be a part of *Saint John's* story as well.

SECTION 1

The Problem

CHAPTER 1

Sheila's Impossible Dream

— October 5, 2016 —

***It is three o-clock in the morning**, pitch black, and extremely cold outside along the banks of the river. The slow-moving water makes its way in the quiet darkness from somewhere east to nowhere west. A misty blanket of frost lies thick on the ground, clumping the weeds along a muddy bank. With the exception of the rippling water, it is eerily silent.*

A light from a small, disposable lighter flicks on and off several times, illuminating the inside of a faded and tattered Coleman tent and the sole silhouette of someone attempting to light a cigarette. Sheila Torres is awake. At this time of the night, she is always awake. It's hard to sleep when you're starving, on the verge of freezing, and constantly terrified of who might be lurking just outside. After years of living like this, it's something she had mostly gotten used to, but was never comfortable with.

Nobody gets comfortable with it.

For Sheila, this is the way it had gone most of her life. A good portion of it anyway. Now, at 55 years old, she had somehow spiraled, around and around like an old war plane shot from the sky, falling ever-downward with each passing year. Since the day she dropped out of high school so many decades before, she never stopped falling. So long ago now, she can't really even remember how it all happened or how she got here in this old tent along a river with no name.

Her younger brother had died tragically. –She blamed herself. His death, or rather the absence of his life, left her with a gigantic hole and this haunting sense of guilt so heavy that only booze or meth dulled the pain.

Taking a long pull from her cigarette, she drifts, remembering those days in high school. Fleeting days and faded memories, she recalls only bits and pieces. It meant nothing. There was a boyfriend...Adam something or another...Italian kid. Doesn't matter. Didn't last. Men never lasted. They came, and they went, flowing through her world like the endless river now outside her tent.

Dancing as a hula girl on a sunset dinner cruise was her only real source of income. Everything became so dark, it hurt to be awake. Drugs became the priority. And then she went and lost her job. Evidently, even hula dancers need to show up for work on time.

Barely even 20 years old, she was soon evicted from her apartment, and the brutal, cold world of the street swallowed her whole. Couch-surfing, hopping from one couch to another, worked for a while. But everyone, even so-called "friends," soon grew tired of her. Nowhere to turn, she wandered, looking for anything to eat and a safe place to sleep. There was little of either. Along the way, if she happened to run into someone who might offer a little booze or other painkiller, she welcomed it.

One day bled slowly into the next. The names of towns and cities she stumbled through became meaningless. Her once-hopeful future was shattered. The memories of a mother and father, her brother....faded like an old photograph...all long gone now. A life buried somewhere in a blurry past.

Outside, the sun was starting to come up, making it a bit easier to see inside the tent. Funny how the coming of morning brings a sense of ease, even when you loathe each new day. She had one more cigarette left and decided not to save it. Sleep could wait.

She flicked the lighter several times, finally getting a flame, and looked down at the place where her dog, JJ, used to sleep, there at the foot of her blankets. She smiled briefly, finished lighting the cigarette and inhaled, thinking of the day she'd found him, this scrawny, little, black Chihuahua with that innocent look on his face. Like her, JJ was a lost couch-surfer.

A welcome ray of sunshine for both, they had connected immediately. A pair of castaways. They lived together in a mangled tent, sleeping by the safety of day, creeping out by night, "dumpster-diving" in search of something, anything, to eat. Along the riverbanks and in the hidden back-alleys, she made a few friends now and again, selling what she could. Aside from her addictions,

JJ needed to eat. It was impossible to look at his sad, little face when he was so hungry.

She inhaled deeply again. Thinking about that mongrel now, her eyes became moist. He was the only bright spot in her miserable world, and even he left her. And just like the death of her brother, she had played a role. Little JJ died because of her. Off hustling for booze one night, she left him alone in the tent. Embers from the fire pit must have blown against the side of the tent or something – it was hard to say. Trapped inside, he had no way of escape. When all you have in this world is a tent and a dog, and both are suddenly taken from you in a roaring ball of flames, the pain is unbearable. Almost beyond comprehension.

It was starting to get warmer outside. She unzipped the tent and waved the smoke out of the opening. The sky was lighter gray now, revealing more of the river passing by. She desperately needed booze – whiskey, vodka, anything – but with no cash, it might be a while. She pulled a crumpled leaflet from her jacket pocket and stared down at it. A lady at some rehab office downtown had given it to her, telling her there was this place…Saint John's, and what some were calling "The Red Door." Supposedly, it was some sort of magical place where broken women just like her went in…and came out better. They changed.

This sounded so good. But it couldn't possibly be true. Not for Sheila.

Shoving the flyer back into her pocket, she decided to try and sleep. She laid down, pulled the dirty blanket up around her chin and closed her eyes.

— October 6, 2016 —

The sun had been up now for almost half the day when she finally awoke, During the few hours she slept, the crumpled brochure for that place they called "The Red Door" had fallen out of her pocket. Around noon, it was the first thing she saw upon opening her eyes.

A sign? Perhaps. She still believed in things like angels and miracles... just not for her.

Over the previous week, she had managed to scrounge together a small handful of change;: a few dimes and a quarter from the day before. Certainly, it was not enough to purchase anything to eat, or anything worthwhile, for that matter; then again, it was enough to make a phone call.

Sheila's story continues later in this book. For now, though, let's move forward and open the door a little further into what is happening in our country. As you read, you will hopefully begin to grasp a clearer picture of the people, the policies, and the political landscape, the good and the bad, that have impacted her journey and that of many others profiled in this book. Together, they serve to inspire hope that real change is possible with the proper support and inspiration.

Sadly, the world in which Sheila existed is not all that uncommon these days. Some people might look upon it and dismiss her pain, assuming she pretty much got what she deserved. She had lived a life of complete degeneracy, after all. What else could she expect?

It is such a common sight – more and more each day. The homeless are all around us. It raises the question, "Why are they here, and who are they?"

Many people genuinely care, and if they knew how to change the situation, they would likely step forward to help. The difficulty lies in the belief that there is no hope, that there is actually very little that can be done, and that the problem of homelessness is so big and so far-gone that it's too late. Homelessness is on the brink of becoming an acceptable part of our culture now. Many citizens are virtually anesthetized to it.

What about our government – our elected leaders? Surely, the solution falls to those we have elected. Are there not countless programs funded by our hard-earned tax dollars to bridge this gap? Indeed, there are. Homelessness in America, in that sense, is a multi-billion-dollar undertaking. In FY 2021, the Department of Housing and Urban Development (HUD) reports that it alone will spend over $3 billion on homelessness, which does not include the spending of the 20 additional federal agencies also involved in battling homelessness…nor does it include states and local governments, many of which kick in a fair share of funding as well.

So, what's the problem then? Our tax dollars fund non-profits that serve the homeless. Many programs exist. Why is the problem getting worse?

Unfortunately, the money spent seldom addresses the real problem. As a society, we often spin our wheels treating the symptoms versus the disease.

This is not, however, a book about hopeless problems that cannot be solved. On the contrary, this is an urgent and timely message about the real change needed to reverse the ravaging trend of homelessness. This book provides clarity on the real problems – the ones that lead to homelessness in the first place – so that we develop solutions that actually make a lasting difference. And while the stories you will read are about women and their children who overcame grueling challenges, including homelessness, to permanently change their lives, the underpinnings of their stories apply to all those attempting to lead very different lives going forward, to become who they were intended to be.

Finally, this book calls for dramatic changes. It pulls back the curtain, in an effort to help us see that if we continue to understand and address homelessness the way we have for the past decade, we will experience the same devastating results we see today. Yes, homelessness is spiraling out of control. For those willing to listen, however, real answers do exist.

While traveling across the country over the past several years, people often casually ask me, "So, what do you do?" I usually respond with the difficult summation that "I help homeless women and children become self-sustaining." Every single one of my interrogators, literally hundreds of people – old and young, black, brown and white, male and female, Republican and Democrat – all are deeply concerned and equally confused regarding our country's recent explosion of homelessness.

They all ask the same question, one that, quite frankly, I had not even taken the time to ask myself before I dove head-first into *Saint John's*:

"What is really going on out there to cause such an explosion in homelessness?" And more importantly, "Can anything really be done about it?"

These steady and piercing questions finally forced me to dig deep and begin to search for the answers to their, and my, concerns. It caused me to look back upon the available data, actual homelessness numbers and – as the federal government is the largest singular financier of homelessness programs – at federal policy as well. In turn, it caused me to look further, out into a future in which those who become homeless might actually have the opportunity to improve, thus exiting the system better for it. There are answers. Together we can and must solve this problem. This is not a futile effort. Because we must ALWAYS dream the impossible dream...and reach for the unreachable star.

"THE IMPOSSIBLE DREAM"

To dream the impossible dream
To fight the unbeatable foe
To bear with unbearable sorrow
And to run where the brave dare not go
To right the unrightable wrong
And to love pure and chaste from afar
To try when your arms are too weary
To reach the unreachable star

This is my quest
To follow that star
No matter how hopeless
No matter how far

To fight for the right
Without question or pause
To be willing to march,
march into hell
For that heavenly cause
And I know
If I'll only be true
To this glorious quest
That my heart
Will lie peaceful and calm
When I'm laid to my rest

And the world will be
better for this
That one man, scorned
and covered with scars,
Still strove with his last
ounce of courage
To reach the unreachable,
the unreachable,
The unreachable star

And I'll always dream
The impossible dream
Yes, and I'll reach
The unreachable star

Composed by Mitch Leigh and written by Joe Darion, "The Impossible Dream" is a song made popular by the 1965 Broadway musical *Man of La Mancha*.

The lyrics are strangely relevant toward the effort in solving today's homeless epidemic.

CHAPTER 2

The Red Door

The Journey Begins

A Word from Michele Steeb

As an everyday, ordinary person focused on building a career and making my way in the world, in 2006, I somehow woke up, saw the true problems, and realized... I needed to do something.

In 1985, members of *St. John's Lutheran Church* in Sacramento noticed more and more women, many with small children, sleeping on the front steps of their church. Women and children huddled in the cold, looking directly up at you while you attempt to enter church...that's tough to ignore.

A result of some very compassionate and forward-thinking individuals, a new emergency shelter within a neighboring building, Goethe Hall, turned into *St. John's Shelter for Women and Children* at 5 PM every evening. The shelter grew, but strangely, so did the number of women and children desperate for help. The church volunteers struggled to keep pace with the growing demand.

In 1988, the shelter formed its own independent non-profit, 501(c)(3) organization, hired additional staff, and moved to a facility that allowed 20 more beds (40 total) for the increasing number of women and children in need. However, despite the real underlying issues, it remained only an emergency shelter, opening its doors at night, then closing them again at 8:00 the next morning. During the day, the women and children wandered the streets until the shelter opened its doors again as the sun went down.

Demand continued to increase, soon far exceeding the shelter's capacity to serve. By 2004, the shelter developed a partnership with Sacramento County, allowing it to move once again to an even larger facility. The new facility served up to 100 women and children each day, 24-7, though still primarily focused on beds and meals.

In those days, it wasn't known as the "*Red Door.*" That was to unfold much later. But, if I had any idea of the door that was about to open for me, I'm not sure I would have owned the courage to walk through it.

Thank God I crossed over.

In the Spring of 2006, I made a life-changing visit to this struggling little shelter. Compelled to help and carry on the legacy of my grandfather, who had recently passed away, I agreed to join the organization as a Board member. It soon became apparent to me that the organization was in a dangerously precarious financial position and desperately needed stronger direction. I only glimpsed the proverbial tip of the iceberg, however, unaware of exactly how unhealthy the organization was.

Just after Thanksgiving that same year, the shelter's Board members received a call from our distressed Board Chair, relaying that while the Executive Director was on vacation and unreachable for two weeks, two payroll checks had bounced. In addition, the food truck had cancelled its weekly delivery, evidently because that bill had not been paid either. Adding to the dilemma, the bookkeeper resigned under the stress of it all.

I'll never forget that day. It was the first day of December and a blatant moment of truth. Either I did what had to be done…or I didn't.

I consulted with my boss at the time, the CEO of the *California Chamber of Commerce*. In his kindness and understanding, he offered to match my remaining two weeks of vacation, allowing me a full month to work at *St. John's* and "fix it."

If only he knew. If only I knew. It took more than a month, but somehow, we got the train back on the track. Aside from that, something even more incredible transpired to me personally that cold December. I never returned to my old job. One month "on-loan" turned into an entire year. Then another. And another. And I never looked back.

For nearly thirteen, amazing, life-changing years, I remained at *St. John's Shelter,* helping to build the organization into a thriving and celebrated non-profit and creating a new model for how to effectively address the issues of homelessness and provide real change in the individual lives of real people.

Today, *Saint John's Program for Real Change*, now lovingly referred to as the "*Red Door*" by those who have crossed over its threshold, is the largest, most comprehensive residential change program for women and children in Northern California.

The building of *Saint John's*, however, continues. Not only has the 200-300 person-long waiting list remained constant, the programmatic model gets continually refined to ensure it most effectively serves the needs of the forthcoming women and children.

Over the years, we were often called to replicate our program for men and single fathers. I always responded that we would love to, but given our mission to support women and children, any expansion of *Saint John's* needed to focus on meeting their unique and growing needs first.

The Tipping Point

Shortly after I officially joined *Saint John's* in early 2007, a young woman named Katie entered the shelter with her daughter. A few days later, another woman, Shelly, also entered along with her two boys. I soon learned that Katie and Shelly were sisters, and that 18 years earlier, both of them had lived in the original shelter with their mother.

Wow.

The proverbial light bulb clicked on! The realization struck me that, even though needed, providing temporary shelter and a couple of meals will never break the pervasive, generational cycle of poverty. So, the real answer? *Saint John's* needed to evolve. The organization needed to transition from just an emergency shelter to a full, in-depth program completely dedicated to providing new solutions and real answers toward ending the multi-generational cycle once and for all. We needed to aim our efforts directly at addressing the deeper problems that led these women into homelessness in the first place.

So simple, right?

I remember wondering why our system leaders had not yet come to this conclusion. Each homeless individual is different, each with his/her own unique story. Once an individual is understood, then and only then, can meaningful solutions be put in place, to rebuild lives and teach, as I call it, "The art of fishing."

Give a man a fish and you feed him for a day. Teach a man to fish and you feed him for a lifetime.

LAO TZU

Naïve? Perhaps. Impossible? Not even close.

It became almost immediately evident that by putting these principles into practice, the women began achieving more, their confidence dramatically increased, and a new and exciting momentum kicked in.

Saint John's is no longer just another temporary shelter. Today, it provides a full solution, taking women and their children through an arduous 12-to-18-month residential rehabilitation program. Women find more than just their daily bread. They find themselves. They heal. They thrive.

As time pressed on, the organization aptly renamed itself, removing the word *"shelter"* and replacing it with *"Program for Real Change."* A new logo introduced the symbolic *Red Door*; a veritable entrance to a new world, serving as a beacon of change and hope.

Formerly homeless, single mothers cross over the threshold of the *Red Door* to rebuild their lives through new vocational skills, increased confidence, and the simple, daily, personal habits necessary to "do life" on life's terms. What started as an emergency shelter with the best of intentions blossomed into an inspiring assault on the very roots of homelessness, and a glimpse of the road ahead to effectively attack a problem that threatens our nation as a whole.

Ironically, through the initial process of rebuilding the organization's brand, I found the opportunity to work directly with David Flanagan – someone who would later become a driving force behind *Saint John's,* and now the co-author of this book.

"Once the fire inside burns brighter than the one around you, you will survive whatever comes your way..."

– UNKNOWN

A Man Knocking on the Red Door

A Word from David Flanagan

In the telling of the stories throughout this book, Michele Steeb reaches deep, unveiling the real-life examples she personally witnessed as an integral figure in the success of each one. As her co-author, my own journey with *Saint John's*, however, unfolded in a very different way…one which I never anticipated.

When I was first introduced to *Saint John's*, I felt I needed to "do my part" in an effort to help a worthy cause. As owner of *Misfit*, a company that provides brand development and marketing, *Saint John's* approached me to help clarify its image within the larger community. (That's what I do for a living.) So, as a man who was raised believing that a decent person, certainly a good corporate citizen, gives back to their community, I agreed to lend a hand in their time of need. While most of the stories contained in this book recount the journeys and the dramatic change that have occurred in the lives of others, what transpired was my own transformation.

In the course of working with the organization, I helped develop a new logo – the *Red Door* – symbolizing the change one finds on the other side. It represented the opportunity for a person to "cross over" and enter a new world – the chance to change once and for all.

It is impossible to stand on both sides of the door at the same time. A line must be drawn and a decision to open the door must be made. At *Saint John's*, for the women who make that difficult decision, they effectively wave good-bye to their old way of living.

The color red sends a message of hope. The ancient Hebrews, while captives in Egypt, painted their doors with the blood of a lamb, signaling their faith in God. The Chinese believed a red door wards off evil forces, as did the Irish and many other cultures. Even in America, prior to the Great Emancipation, slaves seeking their freedom would find shelter and safety in homes marked by a red door. In this sense…the *Red Door…* epitomized the goal of *Saint John's.*

As I started working with the organization, evidently my passion and interest showed. I was asked to sit on the Board of Directors, a position I eagerly accepted in my genuine desire to help. But even then, despite any humanitarian interests, I held a hidden, growing sense of hypocrisy that haunted me. How could I pretend to offer "help" to another person when I myself was struggling with many of their same issues?

I had a drinking problem.

Born into a traditional, drinking, Irish Catholic environment, then stumbling my way into the legendary drunken halls of the advertising industry, after years of liberal inebriation in many professional settings and daily client interactions, my habit grew to include drinking with associates at events, meetings, and other business functions, in combination with that all too familiar three-to-four martini lunch…all by myself.

Drinking in this way, became a regular way of life. Forgivable. Common. Normal.

In time, if I wasn't having a cocktail with a client, I would simply "belly-up to the bar" without them, well-oiled by noon. I hid behind the excuse that "it was just business." I was doing nothing wrong. Everybody I knew did what I was doing. They all drank. And for the most part, it was true. But deep inside, I knew I was living a lie. And each time I entered that old *Red Door*, I stood face-to-face with these brave women who had somehow gathered the courage to face their demons and reclaim their lives.

My drinking increased. Still, I held the secret close. But when I was finally arrested for driving under the influence, and unceremoniously tossed in a filthy downtown jail, the truth began to boil over. My reality, front and center now, stood staring me in the face.

Since it wasn't my first DUI, beyond the whopping fines, I was sentenced to community service and five days in the County Jail – a truly frightening experience that opened my eyes even further to the plight of so many of the women I came to know at *Saint John's*. I realized, in every sense of the word, that I was just like them. Their addictions were my addictions. And now their world…had become my world.

My dignity stripped away, both figuratively and literally, I entered the realm of the criminal, the unwanted, the undesirable, the forgotten. True, I served less than a week in jail, lest I feel too sorry for myself, but I saw just enough to catch a good glimpse of the souls who remained behind.

I offered to step down from my position on the Board of *Saint John's*, but Michele emphatically said no. She told me the organization needed me now more than ever. She encouraged me to use my experience, and my deeper understanding, to create change.

I chose to follow her advice. I suddenly saw the *Red Door* not only as the entry point to a new life for others…but to my own as well. A Board seat, a responsibility to engage in the community, no longer drove my commitment to *Saint John's.* My personal desire to change – both myself and others – did.

I quit drinking.

Today, I remain sober and changed. Physically and emotionally, I am stronger now. I found the will to change and the strength to do it through personal counseling, the support of my wife, Karin, and others who loved me, as well as those whom I witnessed struggling for their own change behind the *Red Door.*

Ironically, it was these "hopeless" women who helped me find my own courage to change.

**"Ask and it shall be given.
Seek and ye shall find.
Knock and the door
shall be opened to you."**

MATTHEW 7:7

When the idea of this book first started, over a lunch table of spicy tuna and fried Brussels sprouts, it was the mere conversational merging of two minds (Michele and David) and the mutual agreement that far too many people fostered great concerns over the increasing problem of homelessness and yet held an equally growing sense of hopelessness about what to do to fix it. There was just too much confusion.

Clearly this book needed to become a reality. The words turned into paragraphs, and chapter one soon evolved into chapter two. Then, like Dorothy meeting her friends along the Yellow Brick Road, just ahead and around the bend, Julie Smithey joined the cause. Instantly an integral part of the team, Julie added needed perspective and far more than she ever imagined.

New Friends Along the Way

A Word from Julie Smithey

Before becoming involved with Michele, David, and *Answers Behind the Red Door*, my experience with homelessness was one of sporadic volunteering and donating here and there. When I thought about homelessness (which wasn't often), it was with a feeling of pity and overwhelmed helplessness.

"There's nothing I can really do..."

Having lived much of my life in the world of education, the more I began to learn about homelessness and the real issues behind it, the more connections I began to draw between the two.

Many people believe meaningful reform in education is impossible. My answer has always been the same: when it comes down to it, real change happens behind the door of a classroom when in the hands of a great teacher, one student at a time. Regarding homelessness, the change that is taking place behind the *Red Door* couldn't be more parallel.

Michele understood that real change happens "brick-by-brick," working with one woman at a time and treating her as an individual. I have come to witness how she has been able to take that single concept and dramatically change her corner of the world. Today, after working with both Michele and David in the creation of this book and learning about the kind of work that is being done in places like *Saint John's* all over the country, I now feel a new sense of empowerment to make more informed, more meaningful, and hopefully more impactful choices with my vote, my dollars, and my time.

Profiles of Courage

Real Stories from Those Who Know

In the later chapters of this book, you will read about a number of other incredible non-profits who achieve equally incredible outcomes in the "the art of fishing" approach, who each day model the way to best address this crisis.

As only one of those organizations, *Saint John's* now serves up to 320 women and children each and every day. This alone translates roughly to changing the lives of over 800 women and children each year.

Saint John's holds a limited capacity spread over three distinct campuses – the "main" campus houses up to 230 women and children in two separate residential facilities; a "re-entry" campus houses up to 50 individuals to help women transitioning from prison; and finally the "independent living" campus houses up to 40 women and children in their final phase toward independence.

We mention repeatedly in this book that every woman and child who crosses over the threshold of the *Red Door* is a unique individual, each with her own personal story and varied battles endured. However, this book uses "typical" or "average" measures to provide a general picture of the families served.

100% of the women entering *Saint John's* are unemployed and living at or below the poverty level. The average woman is 34 years old with two children. Most have elevated *Adverse Childhood Experiences* (ACEs) scores ranging from 4 to 6, with many as high as 9. These high ACE scores indicate a substantially increased risk of chronic health problems, teen pregnancy, criminality, mental illness, injection drug use, alcoholism, and attempted suicide, according to the Center for Disease Control (CDC).

ACE scores of 4 or higher have been linked to risky health behaviors, chronic health conditions, low life potential, and early death. For context, in the general population overall, only 12.6% reported four or more ACEs, according to the CDC.

In addition to a shoddy or even non-existent employment history, the women struggle with multiple barriers that prevent them from living a productive life and being a primary provider for themselves and their families:

- 77% struggle with addiction;
- 68% have been embroiled in violent relationships;
- 58% struggle with mental health challenges;
- 52% have criminal histories;
- 50% lack high school diplomas;
- 34% became mothers as teenagers; and
- 25% have lost custody of their children.

More often than not, clients' addiction and mental health issues go undiagnosed, as do their physical health issues, including dental and vision needs. Many arrive without an understanding, or even knowledge, of the health care system for which they often qualify, relying instead on emergency room care.

With this perspective, it is deeply disturbing when the common and largely accepted response to homelessness focuses on a simple lack of an affordable place to live. This book will delve deeper into this issue later, but suffice it to say that while providing a place to live is important, for the majority of people struggling with homelessness, it alone is not the remedy.

Real Answers. Plausible Change.

For clarity, let's take a step back for a moment. When a woman and her children finally find their way to the *Red Door*, they are exhausted, both physically and mentally. They have lived in extreme chaos and fear for months and sometimes years, most often sleeping from couch to couch or on the floor of a cold garage or shed, never knowing when their next meal might come, nor where they might find some semblance of safety or consistency. All feel literally numb from living in survival mode.

Suddenly, upon entering the *Red Door*, the very fact that they now have a safe place to lay their heads for the next 18 months, a warm bed and clean sheets, nutritious meals, a laundry room to wash clothes, and simple toiletries, diapers, and feminine hygiene products, appears as nothing less than a miracle.

For their children, the blessing is even greater. The school bus comes each day, taking them to and from school. Finally in a safe environment where broken souls can heal, they can let their guard down with others like them, and with kind professionals who treat them like decent human beings. The change is drastic and welcomed.

A broken woman, one day at the end of her rope. The very next, timid and afraid, but stepping up to the plate, somehow mustering every remaining ounce of courage, and knocking on the *Red Door*.

Saint John's employs a five-level system of change and, while it offers a full programmatic infrastructure, each woman's, each family's program looks different from another's. However, everyone works on the underlying issues that led them to homelessness.

LEVEL ONE
The First Thirty Days

Considered a "stabilization period," a woman acclimates to the program, learning the rules and schedules, daily routines, personal expectations, even how to navigate the complexity of a formidable 50,000 square foot campus teeming with ~two hundred other women and children.

Depending on the issues that led to her homelessness in the first place, each woman receives professional case management, core classes, and if she struggles with addiction, substance abuse disorder (SUD) groups including *Alcoholics Anonymous* (AA) and *Narcotics Anonymous* (NA). She builds skills in parenting, healthy relationship development, finances and budgeting, and positive thinking – a topic many in her world never fathomed. Basic typing and computer skills are also introduced. A whole new world begins to unfold right in front of her.

With eyes wide open now, she begins to think and feel with much more clarity. In addition, she begins to see that she is not the only one benefitting from this new world – her children benefit, too. An on-site, tailored children's program addresses the unique needs of children from 0-18. They enroll in local schools and start on the road to their own personal recovery. The family grows together.

During this crucial entry phase, each woman remains on campus – except for Sunday – to solidify her new routine. She learns to rely on the positive support network including her "Sister for Change" – another woman like herself, one tenured in the program, who provides a unique level of support, mentorship, and personal encouragement.

Eighteen percent of women do not progress from this level of the program, either because they choose to leave or because they choose not to adhere to the program.

LEVEL TWO
Up to Three Months

In the following days and weeks, over the next three months, something truly magical happens to each woman. She sees herself through a new lens. No longer homeless. No longer helpless. No longer the weak victim. Suddenly stronger and more capable, she exudes a very unfamiliar sense of hope.

Substance abuse education, healthy relationships, and mental health therapy continue, along with case-management and counseling services. Each class and organized activity expand to include additional exercise and wellness opportunities and more life skills training. Alcoholics and *Narcotics Anonymous* groups provide newfound clarity, which leads to enthusiasm. Infectious excitement creates more momentum and spills over to others in the community as well. Life feels more manageable. Success breeds success.

Then, with a growing understanding of personal finance concepts, she finally begins to attack that dark and menacing shadow of years of accumulated debt. Seemingly debilitating at first, perhaps an accrual of tens of thousands of dollars over the years, she builds the tools, understanding, and confidence to create a viable debt reduction plan. And like so many other women before her, a completely unfamiliar light appears at the far end of the tunnel.

With a new and growing sense of confidence, each woman begins the next phase with hands-on employment training at one of *Saint John's* three social enterprises – *Plates Café & Catering, Plates Midtown Cafe,* or *First Steps Child Development Center.* In other words, she begins job-training to learn how to exist and thrive in the working world. Working in this way, alongside others like her, breeds an incredible sense of accomplishment and confidence.

If a woman still needs her high school diploma, as do approximately half the candidates, she spends two days per week studying in a *High School Diploma Attainment* class as part of her new weekly routine.

Family therapy begins; most have never heard of such a thing. Clinical assessments occur, including ACEs. Child care and transportation services provided by *Saint John's* allow each woman to focus on complete healing and personal transformation. Real change unfolds, like the moth transforming into the butterfly. She sees a whole new world filled with never before imagined possibilities.

Level Two, however, is where the real and hard work transpires – where the proverbial rubber meets the road. In this crucial period, each woman learns what it actually takes to manage the daily issues of leading her family, maintaining her sobriety, and being a steady and contributing participant in the workplace.

Although rewarding, women describe this stage as one of the most difficult. As many as 35% of the participants begin to stumble, some deciding to throw in the towel – many who leave early end up returning a second time, after realizing the opportunity they had in front of them. It is a harsh reality. Anything else, however, simply fails to produce real and lasting results. Each woman must truly want to change and must resolve to put in the hard work it requires.

LEVEL THREE

Three More Months

After achieving significant milestones, she is invited to advance to the next level – three more life-changing months. During this time, each woman continues to work on her sobriety, mental health, and the creation of healthy relationships. Now in the final months of employment training, and hopefully with her high school diploma in hand, her primary focus shifts to obtaining and maintaining future employment to generate sufficient income to absorb other financial responsibilities. This is a huge step.

She entertains career options, a truly exciting and previously unimaginable experience. She focuses on creating her – often very first – resume, one that now includes at least one positive reference. Each woman engages in mock interviews to prepare for the real thing. Her savings goals increase to $750 in the bank, as well as continued progress toward any existing debt reduction and resolution.

Her children continue to receive support through *Early Childhood Development and School Readiness Programs*. Her children's school progress is now closely monitored by both mom and the *Saint John's* team.

Progress continues. Hard work is rewarded. Life shows real promise. Again however, like Level Two, this stage also proves challenging, with another 33% deciding not to continue. Again, also similar to Level Two, many of these same women later ask to return, realizing they need the structure and support *Saint John's* provides.

LEVEL FOUR
Three More Crucial Months

Having accomplished more in the last three months than perhaps in her entire life, at this stage she has actually landed a "real" job. Now comes the responsibility and commitment to hang onto it, while successfully managing all of the other daily responsibilities as a single mother, such as child care and transportation. This period tests her emotional strength, courage, and determination.

Less than 10% of the women own their own cars at this point, so navigating both public transportation and the inconsistent child care subsidy system is complex. It's one thing to successfully land and manage a full-time job as a single mother, and an even greater challenge to navigate child care, ensuring your children are well and affordably looked after while employing the public transit system to and from child care and to and from work.

Staff members guide and encourage each woman through each step, along with the positive support network she has built within the *Saint John's* community. With a genuinely caring staff and a group of authentic friends facing the same struggles, this strong network proves invaluable for a woman in sticking to her new routine.

Still in residence on the main campus, the reality sets in that while earning money is exciting, it comes with responsibility. Each woman now pays for a small portion of her overall program costs while maintaining both a savings account with an average balance of $1,000 and her written budget and debt reduction commitments. Finally, *Saint John's* provides credit history and criminal background expungement or clean-up, and the opportunity to join with staff in the search for independent housing.

Approximately 30% of the women do not complete this portion of the program, although at this level, it can often mean they left early for housing, and are well equipped to find employment on their own.

LEVEL FIVE
The Final Showdown

Behold a whole new woman. Through the fifth and final level, a once hopelessly homeless woman now lives in stable housing, within a reasonable commute from her place of employment and hopefully, in community with fellow alumnae for ongoing support. She works full-time with a solid employer. Her children are progressing in school and/or in their day care environment.

Largely self-reliant now, she is not without the "normal" challenges that any single, working mother faces. Only now, she knows what to do. Difficult, yes. Doable, absolutely. Like removing the training wheels from a bicycle, she and her children ride comfortably on two wheels in their independent living setting with continued support from her case manager and/or counselors as needed.

And herein lies the final test. Can she successfully transition to become the primary provider for her family?

For a portion of this stage, *Saint John's* continues to provide her with a rental subsidy, case management, and counseling support, all of which decrease steadily until ceasing entirely at nine months. Finally, with the smile of true success on her face, she enters *Saint John's Alumnae Association*, with women who faced the same odds, walked through the same fire, and came out on the other side whole again. This network provides the crucial, ongoing encouragement and positive support that assists her time and time again on her new path.

"The old, yellow school bus comes every morning to pick up all the children, back at noon with the kindergarteners, then in the afternoon with the rest. These are my favorite, special times of the day…"

— Saint John's Staff Member

Separated No Longer.

Often during levels two and three, many women experience another gift – the greatest gift of all – the reunification with the children previously removed from their custody.

As a result of addictions, violent relationships, and/or the inability to care for their children, approximately 25% of families become separated prior to a woman entering *Saint John's*. So, it's understandable that one of the best and greatest benefits of real change is the reunification of a mother with her children. It is by far one of the most special moments at *Saint John's*, and in many cases, a veritable miracle to behold.

Through her continued commitment to sobriety, to positive relationships, and to hard work, a mother can reunite with her children and, on a beautiful two-way street, the children can return into their own mother's arms once again. It is a day nobody ever forgets.

- *In 2018, 25% of women who walked through the Red Door had lost custody of their children.*
- *Child Protective Services (CPS) is involved and works seamlessly on a reunification plan.*
- *Families come together again, during the program, on-campus together, often after many pain-filled years of separation.*

CHAPTER 3

Not All Succeed

Olliver, the sixth child in a long line of seven, was born in Shreveport, Louisiana to a single mother. With no support from the children's fathers, and little support from her family, Olliver's mom turned to booze – good, old-fashioned bootleg – for the "support she needed." Olliver was inevitably removed from her incapacitated mother and placed into foster care. It became a roller coaster of turbulent change, and by the age of twelve, in and out of more foster homes than she remembers, CPS said there was no better place for her than to return to her mother's care. Only this time, it took her all the way across the country to Sacramento, California.

The damage was already done.

Desperate to stay with her mom "forever" this time, Olliver did everything she could to please her, including making the school honor roll. But on the day she arrived home to share the incredible news of her success, her mother, extremely drunk, responded by grabbing her throat and strangling her. A friend who had accompanied Olliver home somehow managed to intervene; he was the only reason she survived.

CPS immediately whisked Olliver all the way back to Louisiana where, once again, she was temporarily placed with another family. And when that ran its inevitable course, off to an institution she went – the end of the road for kids like her. The foster system did all it could, but the seriously overworked system ran out of places to put her. One of her brothers, older now and in the Military, was stationed in Hawaii at the time. When he got word of Olliver's predicament, he quickly bought her a plane ticket to come live with him.

What appeared as a sorely needed opportunity was in reality a sharp turn down the wrong road. In a military setting, barely 18 years old, confused, and desperate for love and attention, Olliver met and quickly married an enlisted soldier named Victor. Two children later – little Victoria and baby Victor – Olliver felt complete for the first time in memory. The happy family decided to leave Hawaii as Victor completed his military service, and moved to his hometown of Detroit.

However, Victor had a worsening drug problem. First introduced to drugs while in the service, over time he progressed into a full-blown abusive addict. Like it or not, the children had front row seats to it all, including the moment their father was shot and wounded during a drug deal gone bad. They saw it all. Olliver, in a desperate attempt to keep her family intact, and adamant that her children would not grow up the same way she did, endured this abuse for twelve long and tortured years.

Now in her late thirties, the state of Louisiana offered Olliver and her children refuge from her husband, who was wanted in three states by this point. She accepted their offer and quickly moved in with one of her former foster families, who helped her through a divorce and on to a fresh start.

Determined to get her life back on track and end her reliance on welfare, Olliver took a job with an employer that hired people with similarly challenged backgrounds. Through a series of fortunate events, she ended up being interviewed by both Walter Cronkite and Barbara Walters as a "welfare reform success story," and ended up becoming a spokesperson for her new company. All the while, she dealt with two extremely rebellious teenagers, deeply affected by the trauma they experienced while growing up with Victor. Both eventually ended up in Juvenile Hall. Despite her celebrated recovery, Olliver turned back to drugs to cope.

Still struggling to keep her head above water, she decided to return to school and obtain a degree in office administration. Despite her secret drug use, she continued to rise in the ranks at her workplace, while behind the scenes, her home life held an entirely different story.

Her son now in prison, her daughter now a full-blown addict with three toddlers from two separate fathers, Olliver invited her daughter and grandchildren to move in with her. Thirteen of her daughter's supposed friends – all fellow addicts – soon followed. Eighteen people, all living under a single roof, all hopelessly boiling in a soup of drugs, their world spun off its axis and completely out of control.

Olliver finally escaped and found refuge behind the *Red Door*. Victoria and her children followed shortly thereafter. Now with a clear path to recovery and with structure and support surrounding them, they thrived. It seemed they had finally broken free.

Today, Olliver, now 60 years old, is the sole parent to four grandchildren. Her daughter, Victoria, unfortunately returned to her old stomping grounds and the world of meth, dying of a massive overdose in 2018. Her son Victor, finally released from prison in 2019, came home to live with her, but was re-arrested soon thereafter.

On a brighter note, she married a wonderful man named, ironically, Oliver, who loves and supports her greatly.

Continually committed to change since leaving *Saint John's* in 2009, and to becoming all God called her to be, Olliver excelled in school, earning her Bachelor's degree in Biblical Studies, a Master's degree in Theology, and a Doctorate in Christian Counseling. She serves faithfully as the Senior Pastor of *Peculiar Children of God A.M.E. Zion Church* and teaches at *Pacific Northwestern Seminary*. Never forgetting her roots, she taught weekly Inspirational Studies classes at *Saint John's* through early 2020.

— AUTHORS' OBSERVATION —

One Succeeds Where Others Do Not

For a clearer, better understanding of why so many of the homeless struggle to succeed, it is worth revisiting the following data:

A 2017 study by the *Journal of Health Care for the Poor and Underserved* found that among homeless adults in California's Santa Clara County, 78% percent grew up in a household with a person with drug or alcohol dependence, and 65% endured psychological abuse as a child.

It goes without saying: traumatized children grow into traumatized adults, unless their trauma is properly addressed. They will likely continue the same vicious cycle without early and thorough intervention. (The ACE data presented in Chapter 1 also underscore this point.)

"Alone, we can do so little.
Together, we can do so much."

HELEN KELLER

On the day I first met her in 2008, Olliver collapsed in my arms in the *Saint John's* dining room in an attempt to give me a hug for taking her in. At 48 years old and completely emaciated from a steady diet of cocaine, her body had all but given up.

So how did Olliver escape what her children did not?

Olliver's son, Victor, eventually diagnosed with Schizophrenia, never received the therapy he needed to address the trauma he experienced as a child. While the system addressed his family's housing needs as they escaped his father's violent clutches, no discussion of therapeutic services ever occurred. Over his many years housed in prison, no resources helped him.

After entering *Saint John's*, Victoria, Olliver's daughter, showed signs of change. Unfortunately, at this point in the organization's history, it provided little in the way of services. As a result, Victoria missed out on the full array of mental health and substance abuse services required to address the trauma she faced as a child.

Olliver arrived at *Saint John's* during that same transitionary period, but she remained connected with the organization once she graduated – a crucial difference. Therefore, she accessed additional classes, services, and other valuable resources as *Saint John's* introduced them. In fact, Olliver's case helped bring to light the need for several of the services the organization now has in place.

Each time she returned to *Saint John's,* to reconnect and heal herself, many of the newer clients would seek her out for support, serving as an unexpected gift: a great personal satisfaction and joy. Eventually, she enrolled in schooling to provide these same services on a professional and spiritual basis.

In staying connected with *Saint John's* and fellow alumnae, Olliver also remained accountable. Throughout life's regular ups and downs, she remains clean and sober and faces each day head-on with an amazing inner strength and an enviably positive attitude.

As a perfect example of her fortitude, two months prior to this book's publication, Olliver was diagnosed with Stage Three lung cancer, one week after losing her best friend, Frankie. All this unfolded in the midst of overseeing her twelve-year-old granddaughter's Zoom schooling, while caring for her husband, who now struggles with dementia.

Through all the unknowns, the grueling radiation and chemo treatments, Olliver's faith, strength, and positive attitude endure. A powerful role model and shining example for her grandchildren and for all of us, Olliver's story demonstrates the ruthless and unyielding effects of unaddressed trauma as well as the possibilities that exist once properly addressed.

**"Keeping mercy for thousands,
forgiving iniquity, transgression, and sin –
this will by no means clear the guilty,
visiting the sins of the fathers upon their
children, and upon their children's children,
unto the third and to the fourth generation."**

EXODUS 34:7

SECTION 2

The Questions

CHAPTER 4

Faceless People

Who Are The Homeless?

Candidly, I bristle whenever I hear that jaded term, *"The Homeless."* The breadth of people who "become homeless" is just as great as the breadth of people shopping at your local grocery store. Paradoxically, this diversity plays into the hands of the government officials who, in their concentrated effort to make a very difficult job easier, treat every person in this category the exact same way. While I much prefer to use the term "those struggling with homelessness," or "those who become homeless," it is rather wordy, cumbersome, and tends to become redundant. Therefore, for readability, clarity, and simplicity, I will resort to using that uncomfortable term *"The Homeless."*

Who are the Taxpayers?

The profile of those who pay taxes in America is as broad as the *"The Homeless"* category. For the sake of further discussion, however, I feel the need to paint a clearer picture of the average American taxpayer, one that will serve as an example as I use the term throughout this book.

According to the *Bureau of Labor Statistics*, the average taxpayer has 1.4 children and works full-time. This individual earns $49,000 per year and pays approximately $6,800, or just over 14% of their earnings, in federal income taxes,. According to the Tax Policy Center, in 2016 25% donated to charitable causes, and in 2014, 25% volunteered their time.

The aforementioned defines "the taxpayers." I often refer to this term, as well as the "public good" and "society," interchangeably. Even though there is a great span within this group, this "individual" is typically hard-working, raising or having raised a family, with a sizable percentage giving either time or money to charitable causes, all on fairly limited incomes. It is by no means the comfortable millionaire, kicking back on a yacht, with nothing else to do with their time and money.

Through taxes, how much are taxpayers spending to help the homeless?

The Department of Housing and Urban Development (HUD) plays a lead role in policy, allocating taxpayer spending to address homelessness. However, multiple federal agencies manage 33 programs that explicitly flag homeless individuals as beneficiaries. The chart below outlines federal spending on homelessness… which exposes an over 200% increase in homelessness spending since *Housing First* was cemented into Federal policy between 2011-2013:

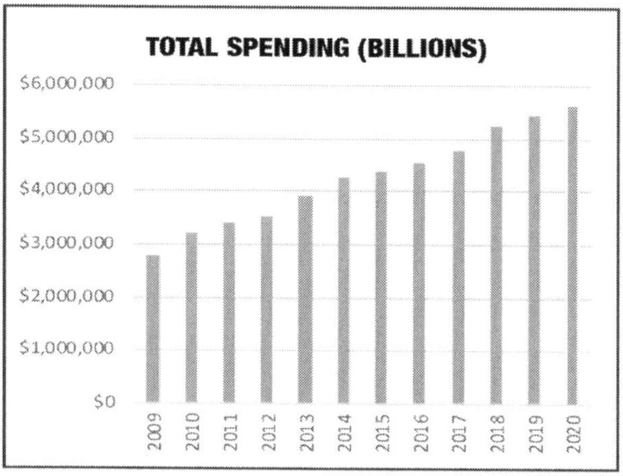

Total Federal government spending (34 agencies) on homelessness – USICH 2020

Federal taxpayer funding, however, is but one piece of the puzzle. States, municipalities, and other organizations also play a large role in providing funds to address homelessness.

In May 2019, the *Wall Street Journal* reported that New York City spent $3.2 billion in city funds on homelessness programs in 2019, on top of about $134 million from federal programs that benefit the homeless.

The *San Francisco Chronicle* reported that San Francisco taxpayers spent $364 million on homelessness in 2019, in addition to the $43 million they were projected to receive in federal funding to serve the homeless.

Private funding – donations made directly from individuals, corporations, foundations and/or churches – is also a significant source of homelessness funding. For example, organizations such as *Saint John's* subsist largely on private donations made directly to the organization – almost 50% of its $7.3 million operating budget in 2019. What's more, *Saint John's* – started on the steps of *St. John's Lutheran Church* – was funded solely by the church during its first three years of operation. In addition, according to the *Cache Valley Daily (2017)*, the *Church of Latter-day Saints* spent $42 million between 2007-2017 to build housing in Salt Lake City for people experiencing chronic homelessness.

CHAPTER 5

Challenging Goliath

In the Fall of 2017, with less than six weeks' notice, the County of Sacramento cancelled their substantial annual contract with *Saint John's.*

Poof! $730,000 gone, just like that.

The contract, held for over fifteen years, fueled by taxpayer dollars, simply disappeared. Completely unexpected and unprepared for, the sudden loss was devastating. The only thing *Saint John's* was left with was the single burning question…"Why?"

The Growing Epidemic

In 2019, *The Washington Post* reported that on any given day or night, homelessness plagued nearly 568,000 Americans. Many face debilitating mental health issues, severe addictions, and difficultly in simply finding something to eat. Families destroyed. Children devastated. What about the land of opportunity for these people? What about the pursuit of happiness? What is the answer for these people? Those in charge of disseminating the largest source of hard-earned taxpayer dollars for homelessness, HUD, promised to end homelessness in ten years under a new plan they called "*Housing First,*" rolled out between 2011-2013.

That's quite the promise.

The Birth of Housing First

HUD rolled out this new plan as a one-size-fits-all panacea. The HUD website suggests *Housing First* as an approach to quickly and successfully connect individuals and families experiencing homelessness to permanent housing without preconditions and barriers to entry, such as sobriety, treatment or service participation requirements.

HUD's policy was then adopted by the State of California in 2016, and by Sacramento County in 2017. Accordingly, any organization attempting to help the homeless became ineligible for funding if they required the homeless to be sober and/or to engage in case management. These organizations could not require the learning of new skills either, nor could they "dismiss" people disruptive to the program. This low barrier approach basically meant handing money to anyone who asks for it – with no reciprocal action required on the recipient's part. Free money. No strings attached.

It may sound sarcastic, even simplistic, but it's simply the cold, hard truth. In practice, it is just plain ludicrous. Not only can this never work, it has proven to be a recipe for total disaster – as homelessness has risen by 16% in the United States since this one-size-fits-all approach took hold (*see chart on page 92*). This approach flies in the face of many substance use disorder (SUD) counseling best practices (78% of the unsheltered population according to the UCLA Policy Lab in 2019; 78% of those served by *Saint John's* in 2018), and also conflicts with many best practices in "Family Reunification" (about 25% of those served by *Saint John's* in 2018).

**"One size never fits all.
One size fits... one."**

TOM PETERS

The Immediate Fallout

After fifteen long years of creating real and lasting results in people's lives, *Saint John's* – the largest program for women and children experiencing homelessness in the region – was suddenly labeled "high -barrier" due to its sobriety, case management, and employment training requirements, and therefore no longer qualified for funding.

Perhaps obvious, high barrier is the inverse of low barrier, or little to no requirements. Suddenly, low barrier became the quasi "flavor of the day," as HUD, the State of California, and Sacramento County implemented *Housing First.*

Regarding *Saint John's,* the County stated the organization also lost points because they only serve women and children – and no men. The lack of logic applied here is appalling when you consider that nearly 70% of the women and children *Saint John's* serves are victims of profound domestic violence.

According to the Department of Justice, male perpetrators constitute 96% of federal prosecution on domestic violence. Given the County's opposition to the screening of males – of anyone entering a shelter or housing program – it effectively endorses an approach that risks exposing survivors to further trauma.

In a nutshell, Sacramento County chose to reallocate money from its general fund – money produced by hard-working taxpayers – to another non-profit agency that requires almost nothing from the people it serves… not work training, not case management, not sobriety.

Please understand, this is not a criticism of the non-profit organization that received the reallocated dollars. Years earlier, like so many other groups, this organization only shifted to a low barrier model to remain eligible for government funding. Nor is it a criticism, to be clear, of any County Supervisors who were elected as stewards of these dollars, choosing how to best spend them. It is meant only as clarification for the taxpayer who deserves to know how and why (or why not) their hard-earned dollars are spent.

On behalf of the women and children whom they endeavor to serve, with years of real data and quantifiable results behind them, *Saint John's* stood their ground, presenting the numbers along with heartfelt, personal testimonials from those whose lives changed permanently, from educators who work with the children, and from professionals with expertise in the rehabilitation of women and in trauma-informed care. *Saint John's* stared Goliath square in the eye and defied him.

And Goliath laughed.

Over years of measurable and lasting change in the lives of homeless women and children, the *Housing First* policy won the battle.

Of significant note, prior to adopting *Housing First* as the new one-size-fits-all, low barrier approach and to validate their final decision, Sacramento County staff invited a Los Angeles "expert" to address the Board of Supervisors in October 2016.

Wait... Los Angeles? Home of the infamous *Skid Row*? One of the largest homeless populations in the United States? A County that, in 2019, reported a 12% increase in homelessness over the prior year, with its largest city reporting a 16% increase(according to the *LA Times* – January 2020)? The County that is home to the City of Los Angeles and that on January 10, 2020, requested that the Federal Government intervene because their homeless crisis had spiraled out of control?

Yes, that Los Angeles.

"The real mistake is the one from which we learn nothing."

HENRY FORD

The Sacramento Supervisors and the County staff followed Los Angeles' approach hook, line, and sinker. Since then, not surprisingly, the county has reported an alarming 19% increase in homelessness over 2017, according to a June 2019 report by *Sacramento Steps Forward.*

Coincidence? Hardly.

And despite its massive failure in Sacramento (and in Los Angeles), the County still adheres to the low barrier, *Housing First* approach.

Measured Outcomes

The County's decision had nothing to do with meaningful outcomes. On the contrary, the only outcome measured by them – and the same outcome that remains in place today – is whether or not the homeless person received a permanent place to live.

Consider the principle of "measure what matters." Under *Housing First*, all of the following are not measured, and therefore do not matter: the homeless who become employed – many for the first time ever – who progress from monthly public subsidies to actual earned income, whose children are regularly attending and improving in school, who reduce their public fines and begin to save their money. The only thing that matters – indeed the only thing measured – is the receipt of a permanent housing unit.

To be fair, if *Saint John's* actually wasted tax dollars and/or produced horrible outcomes, ending its grant might actually be considered good government stewardship. But there was nothing along those lines. Zero.

Instead, the *Saint John's* high barrier approach was criticized for the following reasons:

1) **Screening Clients**. — In a woman's initial interview, a team of professional case managers and counselors determine the candidate's desire for change, in service of effectiveness and outcomes. This screening protects the women and children currently living at *Saint John's* who have faced significant trauma in their lives already. It also protects the integrity of the program itself, and the investment being made by staff (time) and donors (money). This same team oversees an informative screening process that stipulates that those on the waiting list must make an effort by calling-in daily, attending an orientation session to make sure they fully understand the program and the seriousness of the commitment ahead, and attending an initial interview.

2) **Total Sobriety** — Given that nearly 80% of the women who enter *Saint John's* struggle with alcohol and drug addiction, their likelihood to maintain their sobriety in a clean and sober environment greatly increases. Moreover, at any given time, approximately 100 already-traumatized children live at *Saint John's*. Finally, given the goal of employment and the fact that virtually every employer now requires drug

screening, yes, *Saint John's* mandates a clean and sober environment.

Of further note, in 2018, approximately 50% of the women entering *Saint John's* tested positive for alcohol or drugs upon initial entry. They were not turned away; rather, they were required to maintain their sobriety from that point on. During her stay in the program, if a woman does relapse, she is not asked to leave. In an effort for real change to take hold, she receives an increased level of support and services to get her back on track. Depending on the case, this same protocol might be applied for a second relapse as well. However, if relapses continue, then and only then is she referred to another full rehabilitation program.

3) **Too Rigorous** — Candidly, the rigors of *Saint John's* exist because life tenders those same rigors. Effectiveness is the goal. In preparing these women for the inevitable challenges that life imparts, *Saint John's* sets them up for planned success.

4) **Dismissal for Breaking the Rules** – Society provides a set of rules that its citizens need to follow; if not, certain penalties are imposed. At *Saint John's*, to breed success and prevent chaos, women and children follow simple, basic rules and personal conduct to which everyone agrees in advance. All clients receive fair warning that, if rules are broken, a woman will then be asked to leave. This does not include small, minor

offenses. The larger "unbreakable" rules include bringing drugs and/or weapons onto campus, any threats to others, or violent acts.

5) **It's Too Expensive** — In 2018, to support an individual in becoming permanently self-sustaining, *Saint John's* spent an average of $16,300 per individual. Sacramento County staff maintained that this was "very" expensive. Is it? It's a valid point if it's true. When asked what it costs the County to support that same person in the system, they conceded, "Well, we don't really know… It is difficult to measure."

Other counties do measure these costs, as does the *United States Interagency Council on Homelessness* (USICH). In their 2017 report, USICH estimated the system spends between $30,000-$50,000 annually, per homeless individual.

That's interesting.

Using the USICH estimate then, *Saint John's* actually saves the taxpayer-funded system between $14,000 to $34,000 per individual, per year. Extrapolating this to the number of women and children *Saint John's* serves annually, taxpayers actually save between $11 million and $26 million every year – and potentially far more, as families regain productivity, including paying their own taxes over subsequent years.

Furthermore, 25% of *Saint John's* families are in *Child Protective Services* (CPS) reunification – a process overseen by the County. Estimates of annual costs to support one child in foster care range from $72,000-$144,000, depending on whether the child is placed with a family or in a group home. Comparing these costs, *Saint John's* then saves the taxpayers between $55,000-$128,000 annually, per child in the reunification process.

Another comparison, given that approximately 60% of the women *Saint John's* serves have criminal histories, comes via the costs to house an individual in prison for one year. According to the 2018/2019 California Legislative Analyst report, that number is a whopping $81,000. Comparing these costs, once again *Saint John's* provides taxpayers a significant savings...almost $65,000 per individual!

Finally, compare *Saint John's* costs against those of *Housing First* itself. According to the *Sacramento Housing Alliance* report (May 2019), the average monthly rent for an apartment unit is $1,445. In a single unit, using the typical *Housing First* subsidy (about 70% of rent), it costs roughly $12,000 annually to support a homeless individual in permanent housing.

On the surface, one might perceive that *Housing First* is the better bargain given S*aint John's* annual cost of $16,300. However, comparing apples to apples requires peeling back the layers of the potential savings *Saint John's* provides:

1) Beyond year one, *Saint John's* clients who complete the program, gain employment, pay their rent, pay taxes, become independent, and contributors to society on the whole. Given that the *Housing First* subsidy is available for life and that there is absolutely no work requirement for the recipient, any cost comparison must be calculated far beyond a single year.

2) While Sacramento's average rent for an affordable housing unit totals $1,445 per month, affordable housing developments receive millions of dollars in government subsidies to build these units. Any valid cost comparison must factor these subsidies into the cost of the *Housing First* model.

The average woman enters *Saint John's* with a CalWorks (welfare) subsidy of $529 per month. When this same woman exits *Saint John's*, she earns an average of $2,508 per month and has created a savings nest egg!

Metrics such as these are not tracked, nor even considered, under *Housing First*.

CHAPTER 6

The Endless Cycle

With six sons and little likelihood of ever conceiving a girl, Adrianna's mother and father dreamed of having six girls to match. So they adopted Adrianna as a newborn.

Lucky little girl.

She grew up in an idyllic, resource-replete family with a devoted mother, the head nurse of the local hospital, and a father who led a successful career as an engineer. From the perspective of an adopted child, Heaven sent her two angelic parents.

Smart, ambitious, athletic, beautiful, and a natural leader, Adrianna had it all… on the outside. But she felt oddly different on the inside. She looked different than her family. She acted different. Feelings of inadequacy swelled. At age 12, she met marijuana, and they developed into fast friends. Her new form of relief quickly progressed to crack by age 13, then meth by 14. Alcohol naturally followed. Barely even a teenager, addiction governed her life.

"Addiction equals self-loathing," she confesses. "I felt so uneasy, so I just 'numbed' it all away. My discomfort in the family actually prevented me from seeking help from them."

At 15 years of age, she worked at the local burger joint, but only as a means to a very specific end – drugs and booze are expensive, so every nickel she earned went there. Not even deterred by pregnancy, her addiction held onto the best of her. Three babies later, she found herself hopelessly trapped in a world of drug abuse and violent relationships.

Unable to function normally, she lost job after job. Then her home. And finally, the custody of her children. She tried rehab, but it always ended in one more debilitating relapse. Deeper and deeper she fell, into the unimaginable depths of despair, until, at age 34, she entertained death.

But then, the government called. Adrianna was offered a government-subsidized home to fix it all – a brand-new sort of drug. She swallowed it without a second thought.

Suddenly, in the comfort and security of a house, reunited with her children, Adrianna felt free to pursue her addictions even more vigorously. Due to the housing program's inability to enforce sobriety and other standards – the non-profit had morphed to the *Housing First* model to maintain government funding – Adrianna quickly lost control. She became embroiled in a violent, drug-induced relationship that eventually resulted in the removal of her son, Jaxton, by *Child Protective Services*. Her status thus changed from family to single. Consequently, she lost her housing as it was designated for families only.

To someone without a home,
***Housing First* sounds like**
a magic, blue pill.

It's like winning the lottery.
The ugly truth is that this pill doesn't
even begin to touch the deeper issues that
caused homelessness in the first place.
Rather, it increases them exponentially.

Then cancer raised its ugly head. Severely ill, malnourished, an alcoholic and drug addict, Adrianna received a Stage Three cancer diagnosis. At this point, her children were living with their father…somewhere…she didn't really know where. The only thing that drove her at this point was getting and staying "high." From the child so concerned with how others perceived her to an emaciated specimen of a person, Adrianna was quickly withering away, alone and dying.

A Very Dangerous Assumption

Adrianna's struggles with addiction painfully echo the stories of countless others. House or no house, their addictions drive their bus dangerously close to the cliff. Many perish along the route.

HUD believes that once a person has a solid roof over their head, they are then in a better place to seek the help and services they need to address their addiction. But it's their choice whether or not to seek help.

Generally speaking, the addict mindset is NOT to reach out for help. Rather, it is to isolate – which is detrimental for the addict and ironically, facilitated by Housing First in the provision of an independent housing

In his book *Cracked*, Dr. Drew Pinsky speaks at length about *Anosognosia*, a medical diagnosis that revolves around a deficit of self-awareness common with addicts. As a practicing internist in Los Angeles with a specialty in Addictive Medicine, Dr. Drew (as he is known nationally through his radio shows) knows the addicted population well, wrestling with these problems on a daily basis. Based in Los Angeles – an epicenter of homelessness – he particularly understands the effects of addiction on those also struggling with homeless.

"These are my people!" he exclaims. "They know they are sick, but they don't think they need treatment." His book points out that over 80% will adamantly refuse treatment even when it is offered. Thus, the assumption on HUD's part – providing a housing unit for life where an addict can isolate, continue to use, and will likely avoid seeking help – is the equivalent of pouring gasoline on a fire. So, what then? Surely, viable answers must exist?

Doing the Real Work

In 2015, after sniffing around *Saint John's* only to run away due to her fears, Adrianna finally returned. Her cancer now in remission, Adrianna knew she needed help, and besides, she had exhausted all other options. At 38 years old, faced with a "do-or-die" situation, she chose to do.

"I told myself I was ready," she recalls, "but what propelled me most was knowing that if I fell any lower, I did not have the ability to get back up."

That realization shook her to her core. Standing in *Saint John's'* shower one morning, hopeless and beaten, she broke down and sobbed.

"There is in every woman's heart a spark of heavenly fire which lies dormant in the broad daylight of prosperity, but which kindles up and beams and blazes in the dark hour of adversity."

WASHINGTON IRVING

"Get me through this, God," she prayed, "and I promise to honor you for the rest of my life."

Right then and there, amidst the streaming water, something "clicked," and the healing began. She immersed herself in the required routine of the program, attending weekly AA and NA meetings, personal improvement classes, and the seemingly mundane chores. Slowly, day in and day out, she emerged from the darkness – yet another butterfly from the cocoon.

Eventually able to see outside of herself, Adrianna saw similar injuries in others around her – something that happens naturally in community, and one of the strongest reasons *Saint John's* values it: strength in numbers. She reached out to others, showing empathy, consoling, and offering encouragement. A gift for inspiring others emerged and quickly caught the attention of staff and program volunteers, who opened the door for her to serve as a peer leader. Some suggested she possessed the makings of a drug and alcohol counselor.

Why, she wondered, would someone listen to a pathetic addict like her, someone who failed so many times in her own recovery? But in her own words, "My mess transformed my message." The incredible depths of despair, the unending struggles with addiction, everything she endured, equipped her to reach others in her same shoes.

She regained custody of her children at *Saint John's*, working on rebuilding her family while rebuilding herself. She enrolled in additional outside classes that propelled her to achieve certification as an alcohol and drug counselor. She landed a job in a rehab program, got an apartment, even her own car, and for the first time in her life, provided for her family, clean and sober. They excelled.

In May of 2019, she earned a higher certification—a Certified Alcohol Drug Counselor (CADC) certification, another significant accomplishment. The same year, her peers elected her to preside over the *Saint John's Alumnae Association*.

"One of the things I love most about my life today," Adrianna says, "is the opportunity I have to pay it forward, not only in my day job, but in serving the women and children of *Saint John's*. Everything that I went through was a catalyst for becoming the person I am now…the person God always knew that I could be. Once I surrendered myself, I gladly took the hand offered. Everything about my life now is different from the one I experienced before," she says.

Today, her oldest son, Marcus, is studying to become an electrician. Her daughter, Gloria, is aiming for the heights of a registered nurse. And her youngest son, Jax, is flourishing both in home and at school. At 40 years old, Adrianna broke what likely would have been a devastating cycle for her whole family. She overcame the darkness.

Like that beautiful butterfly, Adrianna has completely, miraculously transformed – a woman who now knows how to fly, and a future filled with new, beautiful, and limitless possibilities.

— AUTHORS' OBSERVATION —

A Systematic Metamorphosis

Addiction destroys everything and everyone in its path. Kimberly Johnson, the former director of the federal *Substance Abuse and Mental Health Services Agency* (SAMHSA) stated, "There is nothing magical about the 28-day rehab stay to which most patients are limited. It is certainly not scientifically based."

Many government-funded rehab facilities have blindly adopted the 28-day insurance company-based approach and face the added pressure of staggering waitlists which leave them little room to provide the extended time required. Not only insufficient in terms of length of stay, for those in the homeless community, the short-stay mentality forces a return to the very place their addiction took hold – sometimes a dysfunctional home, but often the streets, where they face the cold realities of addiction and the impossible task of staying sober while everyone around them is using. Over and over and over, the cycle repeats. Discouragement and depression increasingly rule, since a once hopeful recovery appears far beyond reach.

A select few find their way to another program offering a bit more time to adjust to being clean. An even more select few find their way to a program that instills sobriety and teaches them how to "do life" sober – how to work, how to parent, and how to manage conflict without the crutch of drugs or alcohol.

Thankfully, Adrianna found herself in the select few. Hanging onto a thread of her faith, combined with *Saint*

John's unorthodox system designed for real results, saved her life, as well as the lives of her children.

Drug addiction, homelessness, and shattered families are not a hopeless cause. They do, however, call for more than a superficial Band-Aid.

"It is an absolute human certainty that no one can know her own beauty, or perceive her own worth, until it has been reflected back... in the mirror of community."

JOHN JOSEPH POWELL

Community, one of the missing puzzle pieces in the current system, plays a crucial role in determining success, especially for addicts, who tend to isolate. To engage with others who face the same struggles, in a guided, controlled environment, serves as a remedy in and of itself. Community provided Adrianna a lens through which she saw the beauty, gifts, and struggles in others, eventually unearthing those within herself. Community helped her feel safe for the first time, no longer in this world alone. It encouraged her to take one step, then another. The steps turned into brisk walks that soon turned into her reaching heights beyond what she imagined.

After successfully graduating the program, Adrianna continued to build and support community, stepping up to run the *Saint John's Alumnae Association* along with five of her program peers.

"I would not have survived any other way," Adrianna claims. "It made the difference."

Addicts tend to isolate, draw the curtains, and rely upon their own devices. Some argue they have a right to do so, yet medically speaking, allowing a homeless addict to retreat to a place where "nobody is looking," and where nobody holds you accountable, seems analogous to assisted suicide… at taxpayers' expense. In plain speak, it is a bus ticket down the road to failure.

Consider the life Adrianna would now be missing out on, consider where her children would be, and consider the untold losses created for the hundreds of others she has since helped as a drug and alcohol counselor and as an *Alumnae Association* President. One might argue it is almost criminal any other way.

Drawing the Right Conclusion

Adrianna's story illuminates the flawed thinking behind the *Housing First* approach for those struggling with addiction, including the conclusion that "a permanent home in and of itself is the answer." In between Adrianna's first and second experience with *Saint John's*, she (temporarily) enjoyed the promise of a permanent home through a *Housing First*-based housing program. However, the majority of her neighbors actively used drugs – an expression of their "freedom" to live however they wanted. Can a former addict maintain their sobriety in this kind of environment? A deadly cocktail for everyone involved, its victims extend well beyond Adrianna.

HUD's mandate to provide a housing unit to addicts, in an environment where sobriety and work requirements are strictly prohibited, creates fertile soil for the disease of addiction and dependence to grow and spread. An addict with nothing but idle time on her hands, surrounded by other addicts in the same condition – it's no wonder Adrianna succumbed to her addictions once more.

"I didn't fail the test, I just found 100 ways to do it wrong."

BENJAMIN FRANKLIN

CHAPTER 7

The Big Lie

HUD originally rolled out *Housing First* in 2008 to treat a small and distinct segment of the homeless population – the severely addicted, mentally ill, chronically homeless – 15% - 25% of the total homeless population as referred to later in this book.

Under this policy, HUD directed all agencies and non-profit organizations that received HUD funding to provide these homeless groups with a permanently subsidized housing unit. As discussed earlier, this low barrier approach prohibited any requirement of sobriety and/or personal accountability. Their logic? The "street homeless" might be willing to leave the streets, if taxpayers provided them with a housing unit where they can continue their "street" behaviors.

From 2011 to 2013, without any reasonable evidence underlying it, HUD applied the Housing First approach to ALL segments of the homeless population, not just the chronically homeless. As shared in Chapter Four, they funneled ungodly amounts of taxpayer dollars into this program – a 200% increase in taxpayer spending since the "one-size-fits-all" roll-out of *Housing First.* Additionally, HUD created a deeply rooted and self-serving layer of bureaucracy to govern this new program: *Continuum of Care* boards. This infrastructure completely obscures accountability for results by adding additional layers of bureaucracy and further dilutes available funding.

Under *Housing First,* HUD effectively divorced housing from human services such as mental health and addiction treatment. What's more, if a housing recipient desires these services, HUD will not fund them.

Yes, select non-HUD-funded services for the homeless exist, depending on location. For instance, large cities tend to have more human services available, however, these services tend to be more crowded, acting as a deterrent for many. Public transportation in the cities, while not free, tends to make services more accessible. Rural communities, however, tend to have fewer human services, if any, spread out over a much larger geographic location, with public transportation very limited, if available at all. Most communities exist somewhere in between the two ends of this spectrum.

The graph on the following page illustrates the incredible challenges homeless people face in accessing needed services.

CHALLENGES WITHIN THE CURRENT SYSTEM

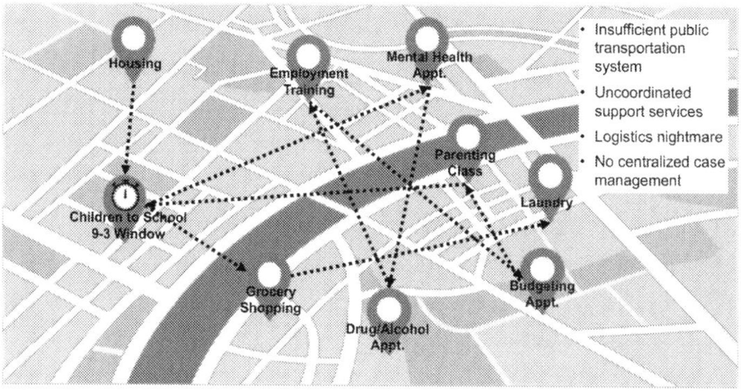

To clarify the dilemma, let's say you are homeless and are one of the few addicts not suffering from *Anosognosia* (a deficit of self-awareness). You choose to get help for your addiction or one of the many other underlying issues you face. Under the federal government's *Housing First* model – which completely divorces housing and services from each other – getting the help you need becomes overwhelming. Even for the highest functioning homeless person, it seems almost impossible when it takes a couple of hours to get from your housing to the service(s) and back again, plus the appointment time for the service itself. The system, as currently constructed, is extremely inefficient and intimidating, especially for those faced with mental illness. No wonder their underlying issues so often go unaddressed. No wonder they remain stuck in homelessness. And no wonder the crisis continues to grow!

Think of our current system like a 1,000-room hotel, not in the way elected officials consider hotels as a solution in the pandemic, but as a regular hotel with an everyday, steady stream of people checking in. Unfortunately, however, none check out. The hotel quickly runs out of rooms. But people still pour through the front doors, lining up in the lobby, spilling into the hallways and out onto the street and down the block, all waiting in the hope of a room becoming available. But none ever do. Everybody who checks in, just stays. Meanwhile, the crowd continues to grow, the people in line growing increasingly frustrated and unruly while their problems remain unchanged.

"Welcome to the Hotel California...
You can check out any time you like,
but you can never leave."

THE EAGLES

How is it working?

Whether you live in an urban area, the suburbs, or in a rural community, all have seen marked increases in homelessness. An October 7, 2019 *USA Today* article revealed the number of people struggling with homelessness increased in 48 major cities across the country – for the first time in years for the majority of those cities. *National Public Radio,* in their July 4, 2019 report, revealed significant increases in rural homelessness amongst children, citing an 11% increase in the 2016-17 school year over the 2013-14 school year.

These increases occurred before COVID-19 hit, and during a time that our country enjoyed unprecedented economic success. From a purely financial standpoint, it makes no sense. Even more confusing, HUD promised *Housing First* would end homelessness within a decade. Adding a little more salt to the wound, HUD and a handful of other agencies used the steady increase in homelessness to convince Congress to allocate more money, which resulted in the 200% increase in funding over the past ten years.

Think of it this way: Congress spends taxpayer dollars funding a given agency to solve a problem. That agency then rolls out a solution. If the problem continues to grow, so does that agency's pocketbook. If a normal business operated in such a way, suffice it to say that it wouldn't remain a business very long.

Congress needs to hold HUD accountable! Americans, in turn, need to hold their members of Congress accountable as well.

The following chart clearly illustrates what happened as *Housing First* was rolled out as HUD's one-size-fits-all solution in 2011-2013:

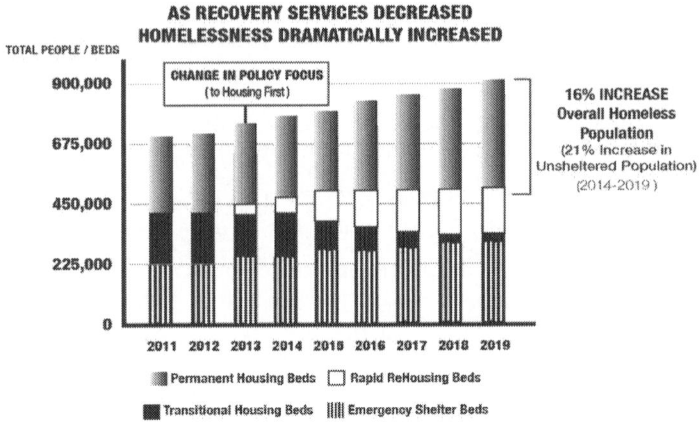

"Doing the same thing over and over, but expecting different results – the definition of insanity," is a philosophy which the State of California has practiced.

In 2016, California adopted HUD's *Housing First* policy as its one-size-fits-all approach. Within three years, homelessness skyrocketed.

- **Statewide homelessness rose** by 16.4% over the year prior, according to a December 21, 2019 *Washington Post* report.
- **In Los Angeles, homelessness increased 16%** over the year prior, according to a January 2020 *Los Angeles Times* report.
- **In San Francisco, homelessness swelled 17%** over 2017, according to a *San Francisco Chronicle* report in 2019.

- **In Sacramento, homelessness exploded 19%**, according to *Sacramento Steps Forward* report in June 2019.

Policymakers and advocacy groups tend to blame a lack of affordable housing for the uncontrolled mushrooming of homelessness. But just as no singular solution to homelessness exists, no singular cause exists either.

For the most part, the officials making these decisions have good intentions. But their decisions have massive ramifications and have largely been made based on false assumptions. HUD made several of these false and destructive assumptions in their institutionalization of *Housing First.*

FALSE ASSUMPTION 1
The Primary Cause

Housing First incorrectly assumes homelessness is a primary condition – that "I am homeless because I don't have a house." The logic seems sound, and government data historically backed it up – until now.

Googling government data on this topic leads one to believe that 25-40% of the homeless population struggle with addiction and/or mental illness. In July 2011, a federal agency that often works closely with HUD – the *Substance Abuse and Mental Health Services Agency* (SAMHSA) – reported HUD data showing that 26.2%

struggle of the homeless struggle with mental illness and 34.7% with substance abuse.

However, on October 7, 2019, the *Los Angeles Times* issued a report that found significant flaws in HUD's methodology to track the data, such as addiction and mental illness, that supposedly validated its narrative that housing is the answer.

Referring back to a 2019 *UCLA Policy Lab* study – one that cited that 78% of homeless adults struggle with mental illness and that 75% of homeless adults struggle with substance abuse disorders – one must ask the following questions:

Is HUD making a false assumption?
Or are they purposefully skewing data?

You decide. In either case, I think it is important to step back and look at the homelessness population on a bell curve. About 20-25% – the severely chronically homeless – reside on the far left of the curve. These are, most often, single adults struggling with significant mental illness and addiction.

The right side of the curve represents those who maintained life on the edge (for the most part), but then fell over as sudden tragedy struck. Perhaps, due to a health issue or layoff, the household's primary provider lost their income and as a result, their housing.

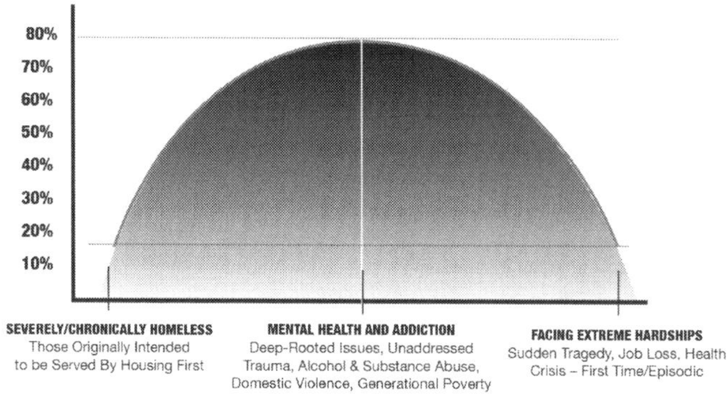

(Of great concern, I fully expect the right-side group to grow significantly, perhaps even double, as a consequence of the COVID-19 pandemic).

For a significant majority of the homeless population (the 60-70% in the middle of the bell curve), their homelessness relates more often than not to unaddressed traumas, further complicated by substance abuse, domestic violence, emotional and mental health challenges, and the vicious cycle of multi-generational poverty.

Recent research by the *Journal of Health Care for the Poor and Underserved* (Volume 28 February 2017) found that homeless adults in Santa Clara County, California reported severely traumatic childhoods, reinforcing the UCLA *Policy Lab* findings shared earlier:

- 78% grew up in a household with a person experiencing drug or alcohol dependence;

- 64.6% endured psychological abuse as a child; and

- 37.5% experienced homelessness as children.

The harsh reality? Under *Housing First,* taxpayers underwrite subsidized-for-life housing for the hundreds of thousands of people in the middle of the bell curve who could – with proper tools and incentives – eventually work, pay for their own housing, and contribute to the communities in which they choose to live.

The loss of human potential under this broken policy incites both tears and anger. Under *Housing First,* we are effectively saying to all those stuck in the middle of the bell curve that they are destined to the same lot in life forever. They needn't bother to aspire to anything more than a subsidized home for life.

Imagine walking into a doctor's office and confiding that you struggle with an increasing dependency on alcohol or drugs. It fuels both health and personal problems. Your work and home life suffer and you risk losing your job and your marriage.
Plus, you can't sleep.

Then, imagine this doctor examines you, determines your liver is broken and that you suffer from addiction. But not to worry –she has the perfect cure. "I prescribe you…a permanent house!"

In utter disbelief, you'd likely get up, walk out of that office, and hopefully, file a malpractice claim!

FALSE ASSUMPTION 2
One Size Fits All - A Narrow Definition

If *Housing First* works for one homeless person, it will work for every homeless person, and their children. Not true.

Housing First policy conflicts with substance abuse disorder best practices, by prohibiting shelters and housing programs from mandating a clean and sober environment. And it refuses to acknowledge the data that an abusive person who continues to engage in substance abuse is more likely to continue violent behavior.

According to a joint study by the *Harvard Medical School and SAMHSA,* released in March 2017, traumatic experiences and their sequelae tie closely into behavioral health problems, warning that those who experienced trauma, including domestic violence, NOT be exposed to further trauma. *Housing First* conflicts with a core principle of trauma-informed care, given that shelters and housing programs are **not allowed** to screen people prior to entering their program. In fact, they are required to accept anyone who wants in, even those with untreated mental illness or addiction, who, also due to *Housing First,* need not seek treatment to address those issues. This policy, and its supporters, knowingly put already-traumatized people at significant risk of exposure to additional trauma.

The Definition of a Homeless Family

HUD employs a narrow and unrealistic definition of homeless families, resulting in hundreds of thousands of children, and their parent(s), being excluded from the homelessness Point in Time (PIT) count and thus the available resources that result from being "counted" as homeless.

With the grossly narrow definition of homelessness put forward by HUD, many families in need are not considered "homeless" enough.

Accordingly, these families are excluded from homelessness counts, rendering them ineligible for shelters and housing programs funded by HUD.

For instance, under its homeless definition on their website, HUD does not consider a family that is "couch-surfing," "floor-surfing," or "garage-surfing" to be homeless because they have a roof over their head. HUD also excludes the families who are somehow able to scrape together the money to pay for their own motel room. In a wicked twist, if government dollars are used to underwrite their motel room, suddenly, these same families are considered homeless.

Based on this unrealistic definition, in its 2019 annual homeless assessment report, HUD claims family homelessness is declining. Using the *U.S. Department of Education's* more realistic definition of family homelessness that includes families with a temporary roof over their heads, the real numbers evoke a frightening reality. Data on the *Federal Department of Education's* website confirms that well over 1.5 million public school students experienced homelessness during the 2017-2018 school year – a staggering 33% increase over the 2010-2011 school year.

Confronted with their unrealistic definition, HUD ignored what is in the best interest of children and families.

According to a piece in the *New York Times* on September 15, 2008, HUD opposed expanding their definition of a homeless family because the "limited" funding available would then be spread across a greater population. False assumption or purposefully skewed data?

You decide.

FALSE ASSUMPTION 3
Real Numbers Don't Lie.

HUD claims *Housing First* is "evidence-based." Not only do the significant increases in homelessness across the country, both visible and not visible, put this assumption into question, a complete reversal of facts merits strong consideration.

Once lauded by *Housing First* advocates as their shining star, the State of Utah initially reported that under the *Housing First* approach, its homeless population declined by an impressive 91% through 2015. According to a December 2018 *Associated Press* report, however, the state's Legislative Auditor General found that "flawed data" led to the reported decline. In fact, the corrected data then showed the homeless population in Utah nearly doubled over that period.

What is NOT measured by HUD to determine *Housing First's* success is also of great concern. Common sense would suggest an effectiveness measurement. Examples of effectiveness include long-term housing stability, earned income increases, public subsidy decreases, lower health care costs, lower crime rates, and more. But according to HUD's Measure 7b report in July 2016, a single metric was employed: *Did the individual placed in permanent housing remain in that housing for six months?*

Preposterous, but unfortunately true.

Not only is there no long-term measurement of those placed in permanent housing, HUD employed inadequate "evidence" to support the one-size-fits-all rollout of *Housing First*, with a short-term study of a couple hundred families called the "*2014 Family Options Study.*"

Supporters quickly seized on this narrow study finding that rapid rehousing, a form of *Housing First*, was less expensive than the alternatives on a per-month basis, even though an earlier analysis undermined this conclusion. HUD conveniently glossed over the most important finding – "There was no reduction in the number of families that slip back into homelessness under this approach."

Let's take a closer look at some real-life examples – people who have faced incredible challenges, individuals and families who overcame significant trauma, battled addictions and mental illness, and through a great deal of hard work, made it through the fire to become the women they were always intended to be.

If anyone knows the answer, perhaps it is them.

SECTION 3

The Answers

A New Set of Values

We cannot cast stones at the current approach to homelessness without providing alternative answers. However, we cannot even begin to determine those answers without first clarifying and defining the core values by which those answers are to be measured. In studying the *Housing First* approach, I still cannot determine what the values are behind it, other than getting someone under a permanent roof. Clearly, that is not a value, merely a box checked, and therefore we as a country cannot determine its true success or failure.

Due to the complexity of the individuals within the homeless population, and the complexity of the problem itself, the answer must include multiple approaches, versus a one-size-fits-all solution – which is no answer at all. Just as *Housing First* is not the sole answer, *Saint John's* is not the sole answer, either. However, the women who have emerged from homelessness through *Saint John's* provide important lessons to be learned.

The stories shared in the remainder of this book outline the struggles and hardship they endured, from growing up all the way through transformation. And though the following stories may appear somewhat redundant, they are anything but. Each story includes unique nuggets that point to real answers. Moreover, each story demonstrates there actually is a way out of homelessness, even for those mired in it for years.

At *Saint John's*, each woman commits to change by following a list of clearly stated values that label the hallways and are ingrained in other aspects of the program as well. These "keys" to success appear visually on motivational wall posters, in class curricula, on staff lanyards, and in monthly client and staff member awards that celebrate the demonstration of these values.

Love
Unconditional acceptance, combined with compassionate truth-telling, within a system of accountability

Courage
Facing uncertainty with determination, in spite of fear

Effort
Taking action and working hard to improve our lives and the lives of others

Gratitude
Recognizing the gifts within, and expressing thanks for the opportunities and contributions provided by others

Respect
Caring for ourselves, being sensitive to others, and embracing differences

Community
Supporting and encouraging each other to be our best

Growth
Attempting new things, recognizing what does and does not work, and continually learning

CHAPTER 8

The Power of Community

On Christmas Day 2015, Mandy, balled-up and writhing in the far corner of a meth house, begged God to end her life. She had convinced herself that her six children, four of whom were living in foster homes, were better off without her. At the same time, the thought of life without them was painfully unbearable. But she had hit rock bottom, waking up only to numb herself with meth to face one more day.

Her eyes slowly closing, falling back to sleep, a knock at the door suddenly stirred her. After searching for six months, her nephew had finally found her, and had come to take her back home.

He brought her to the house of his mother (Mandy's sister) where she struggled for two solid weeks, detoxing on the living room couch. Struggling against the pain, she described it as swimming through the fires of hell. Watching her ordeal and worried sick for her safety, her sister convinced Mandy to check into a rehab program. During her stay there, Mandy regained her sobriety and a semblance of clarity. But where and how to begin picking up all the broken pieces of her life, let alone how to put them back together, was more than daunting. She prayed. She pleaded for guidance. She begged for any kind of direction, even a simple sign from above.

Then, while waiting in the lobby of the rehab center, she glanced down at something that caught her attention – a small brochure lying on a table. Nothing fancy, there was just something special about it that made her decide to pick it up.

Real Answers. Lasting Results.

At an incredibly low emotional state, Mandy was desperate for answers – any answers. If at that point she received a call offering her a "no strings attached," life-long apartment, Mandy says she would have jumped at the chance.

"Housing for life…are you kidding? Sign me up! I may be a junkie, but I'm not stupid." Looking back now, however, she quickly adds, "And I'd be stone cold dead because of it."

The truth is, if Mandy had the ability to get out of her dire situation, she surely would have. But after decades of trauma, drug abuse and chaos, thinking clearly and thinking long term elude the addict at this point. So, the offer of lifelong housing – a "gift" with no strings – feels like an incredible jackpot. Clear in her thinking today and understanding what she needed at that point in her life, Mandy says it would have been "a deal with the devil."

Nothing worthwhile in life is free or easy. It appears that way sometimes, but with poverty, homelessness, and addiction, turning one's life around is complex, nonlinear, and time consuming. Real change happens by doing the hard thing. Real success lies not in avoiding the difficult parts, but in learning how to manage them better.

This concept eluded Mandy at first. But after reading a compelling story of recovery in the brochure she found in the rehab lobby, Mandy received the sign she prayed for. She knew deep in her gut that *Saint John's Program for Real Change* was the right direction. When she knocked on the *Red Door*, not only did she find a safe place to lay her head, she found a completely unexpected opportunity and real answers.

Through counseling and support, she learned coping mechanisms within the very first month, as she now lived with about 200 women and children. They, however, understood and encouraged her. Her sense of confidence grew. She soon experienced the very unfamiliar feeling of hope. All of this in just one, short month.

She felt propelled to continue, to make more changes, even to begin the steps toward reuniting with her lost children. Over a very short period of time, but with an incredible amount of effort and a few bumps and tears along the way, Mandy found herself leading the charge for a whole new life.

She maintained her sobriety, and worked her program. *Child Protective Services* closely monitored her progress, and a Judge eventually approved reunification with her children. Mandy and her children moved into the *Finding Nemo* room, large enough for her whole family.

In the Fall of 2016, just one year from laying on that cold and dark meth house floor, Mandy – a woman formerly with no hope and ready to give up – got a job. Clean and sober, reunited with her children, and now with a full-time position at *Orepac Building Products*, she began making real money – her own money. Talk about a confidence-builder. Talk about hope. Talk about real change!

"Yes, I did the hard work,
and believe me it was hard.
But it was the people of Saint John's
who saved my family
...and my life."

— MANDY

Mandy struggled to look at herself in the mirror when she first entered *Saint John's*. In those early stages, shame riddled her – for the way she had lived, for the things she had put her children through. The love and encouragement shown to her, however, by fellow clients and staff, gave her the strength to consider making the effort. At the end of the day, this support served her in a way almost nothing else had. One of the most important things Mandy needed to heal was love – Unadulterated, unconditional, real love.

She didn't need a subsidized house for life. She needed someone to genuinely love her so that she could learn to love herself, and learn to show her children that same love in return.

A Love Note

Written by Mandy's Daughter

My mother is the biggest inspiration in my life. As much as I am inspired by all the changes she has made and all that she has done to better herself, both for herself and her children, they are not the main reasons she inspires me. She inspires me in that she wants me to do greater things than she ever did.

That's an amazing gift for a mother to give to her child. In return, I want to pass it on. The life she has tried so hard to give me makes me want to take charge of it and continue to make it better. When I tell her this, it makes her happy because that's all she ever wanted for me. Like many parents, she struggles with the idea that her children could ever forgive her for all the "negative" things she's put us through over the years (as mothers do), and still love her in the end.

"I'm your daughter," I remind her. "That's my job."

———

**I have decided to stick with love.
Hate is far too great a burden to bear."**

MARTIN LUTHER KING, JR.

CHAPTER 9

Courage of a Lion

At the far corner of her desk, piled high with file folders and other important documents, the phone rings, demanding attention. Jennifer finishes one last gulp of coffee, sets her cup down, adjusts her collar, and answers it with a smile.

"Good morning, this is Jennifer, how can I help you?"

Seeing Jennifer in action is impressive. At 48 years of age, Jennifer, an integral part of a bustling property management firm for three years now, is sharp and quick to solve problems – a career woman on the go. But in the chronicle of her life, this is but one chapter of many darker ones. The Jennifer of yesterday is utterly unrecognizable.

Not so long ago, Jennifer walked the streets by night, and slept on park benches during the day. It was safer that way.

Nobody actually *chooses* to live that way; she felt she had no other option. Following one bad decision after the next, she sensed she was reaping what she sowed.

Her parents, "functional" drug addicts from the very start, modeled bad decisions. She watched and learned. Raised in a cruel world of unimaginable neglect, fear, and confusion, her father abruptly left when she was twelve, never to return. A hopeless, drug-crazed mother remained.

At fifteen, Jennifer began doing what she watched her parents do – drink heavily and regularly. Smoking dope complimented her newfound drinking habit. At sixteen, she dropped out of high school.

Her mother kicked her out of the house at seventeen. Somehow, with a part-time job at *McDonald's*, she got her own place, where she enjoyed complete freedom. One night, a few friends joined her for a night of drinking. She passed out on the living room couch, and her supposed "friends" took cruel advantage of the situation.

They gang-raped her.

No police reports. No consolation from a trusted counselor. No friends to whom she could turn. Her confidence was shattered. She removed "trust" from her vocabulary. Still just a teenager, Jennifer turned ever more inward to cope. She quit drinking at this point, but continued to smoke weed heavily to numb her pain.

History often repeats itself.

Pregnant at 20 years old, followed quickly by two more children, her partner's drug abuse evolved to physical abuse, with Jennifer as his constant outlet. Accordingly, they became a CPS case. Soon thereafter, she and her children witnessed a violent murder on their doorstep in its entirety. With three children now looking to her for a semblance of comfort, Jennifer packed up her children and ran.

She could not, however, run from the trauma she experienced, and continued to use weed to numb the pain. She got jobs, but without the support of family or friends, the single mother of three did not keep those jobs, which in turn drove more moving and more running.

At 27, arrested and jailed for felony sales and possession, Jennifer left her children with a friend for her 120-day sentence. It seemed to be a turning point. She found a new job, found God through a Bible study, and felt good about the family's new direction.

Then she met a man.

She became pregnant once again. Emotional abuse followed almost immediately. With four children now in tow, she fled again.

She scraped by, accepting odd jobs that allowed her to stay home with her children. During this "still" period, she began to see clearly the effects of the trauma her family experienced, but unsure as to how to access counseling on their limited income, she did nothing.

Her children grew, but they never thrived. Her oldest son was in jail, and her eldest daughter was with her father. Still, two children remained dependent on her for some semblance of a decent life.

Then, while innocently playing basketball in a park – wrong place...wrong time – someone stabbed her youngest son repeatedly, leaving him with severely damaged intestines and a left eye that had to be removed. Jennifer, in no condition to care for him, left him in the arms of a friend. She finally snapped. The constant, debilitating stress and anxiety suddenly overtook and paralyzed her. In a very cruel twist of fate, homeless again at 40 years old, *Agoraphobia* – the fear of wide-open spaces – set in.

Life turned even more cruel.

People passed her on their way to work, shaking their heads and wondering why. How on God's green earth did this poor woman get like this? No one stopped, however, until one day, a passing stranger took the time to stop and talk, telling her about a place that could help her find a job – *Saint John's*. She listened. This place sounded good.

Jennifer first entered *Saint John's* in 2014, but with the sole mindset just to get a job. Due to her struggles with anxiety, she left the program prematurely.

Not surprisingly, she continued to struggle.

In 2016, she called *Saint John's* again, only to be met with a substantial waiting list. Overloaded with women like her, seeking help and a better way, *Saint John's* put her on the waitlist. She refused to give up. She couldn't. She held on to hope…if not for herself, then for her daughter.

She called again. And again. For two tortured months, she placed her name on the long list every day, hoping and praying for a spot. In the winter of 2016, barely capable of making one more phone call, the *Red Door* opened for Jennifer and her daughter.

Now focused on real change, Jennifer knew she needed the structure *Saint John's* offered but admits the rules were very challenging at first. She shared, "My only coping mechanism, smoking pot, was now off limits, as *Saint John's* required sobriety. And I was forced to engage in a very different way than I did in my first chapter with *Saint John's*."

Like a light bulb in the dark recesses of a forgotten basement, it suddenly clicked on. At 46, Jennifer finally found hope. She devoured the counseling and access to education, earning the credits required for her high school diploma. Starving for more, she took every class available, and jumped at every opportunity to advance herself. She thrived in money matters and meditation, embraced the structured routine, and built a new framework to ensure her success going forward.

Through intensive mental health therapy, individually and together as a family, the cruel stains of a lifetime of abuse began to retreat. Jennifer and her daughter healed and grew together, though not without periodic setbacks; a looming sense of anxiety and panic attacks persisted. Jennifer's Adverse Childhood Experiences (ACE) assessment revealed a score of eight, illustrating the trauma she had previously faced. Through additional medical therapy, combined with the emotional support and encouragement she received, they moved forward, step by careful step.

Soon, Jennifer began employment training through *Saint John's Plates Café*, joining many other women in a similar quest for change and renewal. She learned to replace bad habits with new work ethics, developing a set of skills she never even knew existed. She built stamina, confidence, and found strength in real friendship.

Jaja, her daughter, watched intently as all of this unfolded. Her once empty eyes became brighter each day as she witnessed her mother's courage. Jaja too, defiant and frightened at first, slowly began to emerge from her shell. They each marveled at the miraculous change happening within.

On January 27, 2017, Jennifer stumbled across a job opening – a property manager position at an apartment complex. It offered not only a steady income, but an apartment as well. She leaned on her newfound confidence and her growing courage to apply. She worked diligently to prepare herself for an interview. She got the job – one more miracle for which to be grateful.

Today, she and Jaja still live comfortably in that same apartment, and Jennifer continues to thrive in her career. For the first time, she feels she is living.

Not only does she serve on the board of the *Saint John's Alumnae Association*, encouraging and advising past and present clients on the amazing road in front of them, but several alumnae also live within the complex she manages. She provides both an ear and guidance to these women and their children.

"Face change head on," she offers with love and experience. "Commit to this program, and you will receive so much more in return," she says. "My life is proof of it."

Jaja also graduated from high school. She obtained her driver's license and now holds a steady job. Jennifer reunited with her other children as well.

— AUTHORS' OBSERVATION —

Becoming the woman she was intended to be

In 2019, Jennifer received a diagnosis of congestive heart failure. The left valve of her heart weak and barely pumping, she experienced increasing heart palpitations, anxiety, and panic attacks. After all of her hard work and success, this news hit her hard. She persevered through so much, fought so hard, only to be dealt this hand? Jennifer soon realized this diagnosis was a setback, not a death sentence. She realized the world hadn't changed – she had. She took life by the collar and put it squarely in its place.

She relied heavily on her support network of *Saint John's* alumnae and staff who stayed by her side, supporting and encouraging her, along with her employer.

Jennifer now carries nitroglycerin tablets to subdue a sudden attack, and knows how to deal with it. Through regular visits with her medical team, and through her support network that ensures she has the emotional support she needs, Jennifer continues to grow, cope, and to access that deep well of courage she discovered through *Saint John's.* It's a gift that allows her to face her fears, no longer running from them, placing one foot in front of the other. She models how to overcome adversity, how to become the primary provider for her family, and how to care for others in her same shoes.

CHAPTER 10

An Undying Effort

Taking action and working hard to improve our lives and the lives of others

Born in a birthing home for unwed mothers to a 17-year old girl who had dropped LSD several times during her pregnancy, Sheri's first moments were not exactly picture-perfect. Sheri's mom chose to put her up for adoption for a shot at a better life.

Her temporary foster mom, however, left her in her crib for hours on end, rarely holding or nurturing her. Officially adopted at six months old, her new parents did their best to fill the void, a trend that defined their relationship for many years to come. Thankfully, her adoptive father continued his attempts to bond with her, showing her unconditional love at every twist and turn. She grew to adore him. But even so, she never found the courage to tell him her dark secret: Her grandfather – Sheri's mother's stepfather – repeatedly abused her sexually. Frightened and embarrassed, she held it in, and it, in turn, ravaged her inside.

In the 4th grade, her world turned completely upside-down. Her parents divorced. In the blink of an eye, she lost her father while continuing to live with her unemotional, detached mother, who quickly found another man of the house. Nothing like her beloved father, he was mean and verbally abusive, and soon became physically abusive as well. After one particularly violent altercation, Sheri fled to her father's home. Her mother waved it off, never even bothering to come after her.

Now in high school, and with the dark secret still buried deep inside, she turned to drugs to dull the pain. By the time she graduated, meth controlled Sheri. As one addict often turns to another, she became involved with a man who mirrored the others. He beat her. Even through two pregnancies, the abuse never declined. Strangely, two healthy babies resulted, only to face an ultimatum by the state: Lose the husband or lose the children.

Wisely, Sheri chose the former, but suddenly found herself a single mother with a five-year-old daughter and a nine-year old--son. In a stroke of luck, she landed a job on the assembly line at *Frito Lay*. She managed to stop using drugs for a while, allowing her to wake up each morning at 3 AM and shuttle her children to her father's house to get them to school. Good intentions for sure, but it lasted only a few months. A depression shadowed over her, making its way deep inside. One day, unable to get out of bed, she turned to drugs yet again. She just wanted to stop the pain as quickly as possible. Using drugs once again, her already ravaged body reacted quite differently this time. She lost her job and her home.

Eventually, she found refuge for her children with sympathetic friends. She, however, stayed out on the streets, forced to do "whatever it took" to survive. She gave herself over to reckless abandon. Nothing it seemed, including the sale of her body, was beneath her in the never-ending need to "score" drugs. She became pregnant again, but gave the child up for adoption immediately upon birth. The cycle continued.

**"Failure is not in the falling down.
It is in the staying down,
in allowing the setbacks
to define you."**

UNKNOWN

By the time she was 38, Sheri slept in and out of cheap apartments, hotel rooms, and spare bedrooms – you name it, anything to keep a roof over her head. When her father became gravely ill, the added stress required an additional anesthetic. She started drinking heavily. When he died, a steady mix of meth and alcohol soothed the pain.

For two more years she lived on the streets, sleeping in the back of an old, broken-down car. Prostitution paid for the drugs. Dumpsters provided food. She met a man who showed her how to break into motel rooms – to sleep and shower – but his drug abuse proved even worse than hers. What's more, he drew increasing pleasure from purposely terrifying her, including dousing her with gasoline while holding a blow torch in his hand.

Somehow, she escaped.

She survived alone, thanks to her newfound ability to break into motel rooms, entering them late at night, slipping out before dawn. Eventually caught red-handed, with a bar of soap and a blanket, she was booked on burglary charges and sent to jail.

Her sentence included a brief stay at a county-subsidized rehab center. Grateful for the food and shelter, a wary counselor was the true benefit of her stay there. Through their sessions together, Sheri knew she needed "more" than her limited rehab stay.

Sheri prayed.

She didn't know if she believed in God or not, but in an emotionally desperate outburst, she simply blurted out the words, reaching out to whoever or whatever was listening. She got her answer. It was *Saint John's*, a place where women like her were turning their lives around.

She reached for the phone. She called. She cried. She waited.

"Continuous effort – not strength or intelligence – is the key to unlocking our true potential..."

WINSTON CHURCHILL

Having read the previous stories, you probably have an idea of what transpired. Yes, eventually, the *Red Door* opened to Sheri. Yes, she crossed the threshold, and yes, at 48, her life changed immediately. She realized she was nowhere near finished.

She attended classes, particularly benefitting from a course on *Healthy Habits and Healthy Relationships*. She excelled in *Employment Training*. She completed the classes to earn her GED. She worked with a substance abuse disorder (SUD) counselor, attending *Alcoholics Anonymous* and *Narcotics Anonymous* classes. And for the first time in her crazed, upside-down, inside-out life, she found the true difference between learning to "live" sober versus "being" sober.

Filled with a new sense of hope and anticipation, Sheri happily initiated job-search activities and applied for a job that felt particularly appealing. Her self-confidence at an all-time high, she felt she fit the bill well. However, when her prospective employer discovered her criminal record – the burglary charge – they denied her application.

Sheri knew this was the job for her. With *Saint John's* help, she explained the reason for the criminal charge – stealing a bar of soap and a blanket from a hotel room in a desperate attempt to survive outside.

The employer listened. She got the job.

The daily hours spent on that job far exceeded eight. Early each morning, Sheri walked to the bus stop and waited. Every night after work, she climbed back on a bus to head back to *Saint John's*. Two hours on the bus to work every day, and another two hours coming home – far longer than the 15-20 minute drive by car. Four months in, the travel wearing on her, she never lost her attitude of gratitude. Staff noticed, as did the volunteers from *Bayside Church*, very active in *Saint John's*. In front of an audience of over 2,000 people, Sheri shared her testimony. They surprised her with a brand-new car.

"At times, our own light goes out and is rekindled by a spark from another person. Each of us has cause to think with deep gratitude of those who have lighted the flame within us."

ALBERT SCHWEITZER

She felt incredibly validated and indebted for the car and the four additional hours each day it gave to her. She gladly filled those hours driving other *Saint John's* clients – her sisters – to and from medical appointments, court appearances, and other necessary engagements made cumbersome for those relying on the public transportation system.

Employed, with a strong support network – and now a vehicle – forming a solid foundation, Sheri finally felt ready to leave *Saint John's* nest. She decided to move in with her daughter, who needed a roommate at the time. *Saint John's* suggested, and later provided, joint counseling to them to heal their relationship and ensure they could successfully cohabitate. Sheri remained in therapy with *Saint John's* to battle her bouts with depression.

Three years and three promotions later, Sheri continues to work for the same employer. In the Fall of 2019, at 52 years old, she finally moved into her own beautiful apartment. Her grown children visit her regularly, and one of the best parts of it – she enjoys regular sleepovers with her beautiful grandchildren!

— AUTHORS' OBSERVATION —

Ongoing effort made all the difference

After overcoming decades of trauma, abuse, and neglect, most people need counseling to address its effects. Sheri certainly did. Through the therapy she received, as first a client and later an alumna, Sheri healed, learned to forgive, and learned to accept love from the people around her. Her raw determination to see "it" all the way through, to never allow what happened to her happen to her children and grandchildren, made all of the difference. As a result, Sheri changed her life, and the lives of her family members and her family's many generations to come.

CHAPTER 11

A Gift of Gratefulness

Recognizing the gifts within, and expressing thanks for the opportunities and contributions provided by others

Natisha and her two siblings grew up in a very small house in Sacramento, California, along with her mother and grandmother. Her father had vanished long before. She never missed him, because she never knew him.

In 1993, at 18 years old, one of Natisha's uncles introduced her to his buddy: a 30-year old man with a very checkered past. They married that same year. Within months, he wound up back behind bars. In and out of prison over the next several years, he introduced her to crack cocaine, and her world quickly spun out of control. Their mutual drug abuse escalated into physical abuse and violence. After ten years in, Natisha finally escaped.

Unfortunately, as has been seen throughout this book, history tends to repeat itself. Natisha met yet another "questionable" man – the soon-to-be father of her first child, Trevonte. A life now saturated with booze, the relationship quickly mushroomed into domestic violence. Repeatedly beaten, emotionally exhausted, and nearly choked to death, she fled with her son.

At 38 years old, in 2008, she met Joseph who later became her second husband. Around this same time, Natisha's grandmother received a diagnosis of Alzheimer's disease. With her mother suffering from Lupus, her brother and sister both in prison, a severely drug-addicted and homeless aunt, and three already deceased uncles, Natisha was the only one left to care for her grandmother. Besides, her grandmother's apartment offered the perfect place to "crash."

As challenging as life was, Natisha made it work – until her ex-husband kidnapped her son, Trevonte. She tried to get help from the system, but no one returned her calls. The unbearable stress caused Natisha to turn to meth, which developed rapidly into a full-blown addiction, even through her pregnancy with Daeveon, her next child. Her husband was also hopelessly addicted, and as a result they soon lost their apartment surviving through government motel vouchers.

Natisha found herself pregnant again with a third child. She continued to use throughout this pregnancy, too. However, she knew the game well by now, and stopped briefly during her final thirty days to avoid her child being born under the influence (Tox Pos). Jasmin somehow entered the world "clean."

With nowhere to go and kids in tow, Natisha and Joseph scraped together the money to purchase a tent and established a new "home" along the American River in Sacramento. Park rangers befriended the family and tried their best to help them. Especially concerned for their children, given the wet and looming winter ahead, they suggested Natisha consider a 30-day respite program for young children. While there, she took full advantage of the medical services offered to her children, including dental care for her son's rotting teeth. However, when she failed to follow-up on a subsequent appointment request, the respite program was required to alert CPS. Due to neglect, CPS took custody of both children, which Natisha now views as "one of the best things that ever happened to us." Life was not working, and this episode forced them to look hard in the mirror.

Natisha placed herself in a 90-day rehab program, but however Joseph continued to live in the tent and use drugs. A rehab counselor, seeing how desperately Natisha wanted change, suggested she try *Saint John's*. As she learned more, she knew it was for her. She called three times each day – way more often than necessary. Finally, a spot opened.

In May 2017, Natisha walked through the *Red Door,* zealous and eager for change. She took every class offered. She "stepped up" for every request; with over 200 people living on *Saint John's* campus and limited staff, the daily requests for help are constant! Natisha voraciously devoured every tool, every ounce of education, every nugget of knowledge provided.

While called many things in her lifetime, Natisha acknowledges with a smile that "morning person" was never one of them – something very common for those struggling with addiction. But through the rigid structure of *Saint John's*, including the 6:00 AM wake ups, the daily chores, the regular mealtimes and the regular bedtimes, Natisha blossomed into a morning person, building a work ethic that serves her to this day.

With her newfound work ethic, she flourished during employment training at *Plates Café and Catering*. She thoroughly enjoyed her emerging status as a customer and staff favorite on the floor.

Natisha quickly emerged as a peer leader; her razor-sharp wit and her take-charge-style made it inevitable. She led the daily 5:00 PM community meetings with energy, poise, and humor. Her previously hidden talents surfaced like a genie from a bottle – glad to finally be out in the open. Natisha prospered.

With *Saint John's* help, Natisha felt ready to begin reunification process with her family, including her son, Trevonte, who, after repeated physical abuse by her ex-husband, had run away. All her children officially reunited with her in August 2017.

In early 2018, the family – including a sober and employed Joseph – was offered a one-year slot in a transitional living program, allowing them to live together once again. They gratefully accepted, though Natisha had yet to take the final step required for graduation from *Saint John's*: getting a job.

Natisha's case provides an example of *Saint John's* adjusting the services of the program to fits the specific needs of the individual. The willingness to prioritize a person's well-being over a lockstep, one-size-fits-all program makes a huge difference.

Settled and stabilized in their new home, Natisha took that final step. The Career Services Director recommended her for a position with one of its employment partners, *UC Davis Medical Center*. They interviewed her and eventually offered her a career in Environmental Services.

Natisha officially graduated from *Saint John's*. Soon thereafter, she and Joseph married. Joseph's boss paid for their entire wedding and helped them purchase their first car – all as a result of Joseph's hard work, attitude, and dedication.

In early 2019, Natisha's colleague told her about a first-time homebuyer's program. Since neither she nor Joseph had any credit, good or bad, they began in earnest in order to qualify. Six months later, Natisha and Joseph purchased and closed on their first home, purposefully located in an area that was nowhere near their "old stomping grounds."

For those escaping addiction, changing the community and environment with which they surround themselves is crucial to avoid falling back into old but easy patterns.

Also in 2019, Natisha's peers elected her to the *Saint John's Alumnae Association* Board of Directors, a board on which she still sits today. In this role, she encourages current clients and alumnae – women she understands well – to stay on the transformational path.

From tent-owner to homeowner in less than three years, Natisha credits the many "angels" in her life who have supported them to get to where they are today. Natisha says "gratitude" is the word by which she lives every single moment.

"In ordinary life, we hardly realize that we receive a great deal more than we give, and that it is only with gratitude that life becomes rich."

DIETRICH BONHOHOEFFER

— AUTHORS' OBSERVATION —

Gratefulness Made the Difference

Natisha's powerful and prevailing "attitude of gratitude" undoubtedly fueled her remarkable transformation and success. Her infectious attitude not only inspires those around her, it makes them want to be around her, and to help her when needed.

In my positive thinking class, I often shared the following:

"We all need help to get through life. We cannot successfully navigate life without help. People want to help people who—

1) are helping themselves and
2) have positive attitudes.
If you are doing both of these things, you will always attract the help you need."

Case in point; *Saint John's* staff love all clients, but I watched them repeatedly go out of their way to help Natisha. Her *Saint John's* sisters did the same. They simply couldn't help themselves.

I have no doubt that this propelled Natisha's employer to hire her into a field in which she had no experience.

And I have no doubt that it propelled her co-worker to refer her to the first-time home-buyer's program and propelled Joseph's boss to pay for their wedding and help them purchase their car.

A bird perched high upon a branch,
Natisha is no longer afraid
the branch might break.
Her fire is stoked.
It burns bright.
Her confidence lies in her wings…
not in the branch.

Through the dark lens of so many negative experiences, Natisha had the choice to deflect blame for her behavior, to describe life as unfair and too difficult. Instead, Natisha chose to accept responsibility for her choices, to learn, to grow, and to adopt a grateful attitude. In doing so, she forged a new path for herself and her family. The ripple effects…immeasurable.

CHAPTER 12

The Respect Deserved

Caring for ourselves, being sensitive to others, and embracing differences

In a marriage of continual abuse and violence, Alexandria's parents divorced when she was just four years old. The next man in her life, father number two, didn't last either due to her mother's addiction to both drugs and gambling.

Alexandria soon turned to drugs herself. At fifteen, she drank and smoked pot on a daily basis, and soon started selling stolen prescription drugs. For one fleeting moment, she dreamt of attending college, but that quickly dissolved as she turned toward the needle instead. She managed to graduate from high school, but the sterile white halls of a rehab facility supplanted the rolling green lawns of a college campus.

Twenty-eight days later, she found herself back on the street, facing one of many relapses to come. She returned to selling drugs to survive. She discovered her pregnancy, ironically, while in jail. Upon release, one of her only remaining friends left agreed to take her to get an abortion. The friend, however, never showed, which Alexandria now considers a gift from God. She delivered the baby, a sweet baby boy whom she named Izayah.

Even the gift of Izayah could not unchain her from the chaos and destruction that branded her daily existence. At 27 years old, the authorities arrested her again. But in lieu of another failed prison sentence, a resourceful counselor convinced the Court to try a different approach. They sentenced Alexandria to three years in a San Francisco-based program called *Delancey Street,* a rehabilitation program for people with criminal histories. An incredible and purposefully strict program, *Delancey* boasts a successful track record with "her type."

Unfortunately, not with Alexandria.

Based on an inappropriate relationship and possession of a cell phone – both expressly prohibited – *Delancey Street* kicked her out. She returned to County jail to complete the remainder of her sentence.

In jail, she heard about the *Red Door* and shared it with her Parole Officer (PO), who agreed to support her in pursuing it. Alexandria used her daily phone allotment to call every single day, keeping her name on the long list. In October of 2018, she secured a spot. Alexandria served the remainder of her sentence at *Saint John's.*

An electronic monitor still strapped to her ankle, she entered the *Red Door* jumping in with both feet. From day one, *Saint John's* viewed her as an individual with individual needs – and treated her accordingly. Together, she and her case manager plotted a personal roadmap for her success.

"**Saint John's** ***is where my journey truly started," says Alexandria. "Walking through the*** **Red Door** ***was the moment that my faith overcame my fear. I knew I was supposed to be there."***

ALEXANDRIA

The program gradually introduced her to new tools and new ways of thinking and of doing. She thrived on the daily routine and the hands-on employment training at *Plates*. The *Money Matters, Budgeting, Parenting, Alcoholics Anonymous*, and *Narcotics Anonymous* classes fed her and opened her eyes to a world she never knew existed.

"The structure and the rules, including all of the chores, helped me appreciate routine and led to my work ethic," Alexandria says. "And definitely in learning responsibility and accountability."

Alexandria regularly called her son, who lived full-time with her father at that point. Witnessing her progress, her father soon allowed them to visit at *Saint John's*, and not long after, their hour-long visits turned into full weekends together.

"I respect myself and insist upon it from everybody. And because I do, I in turn... respect everybody else, too."

MAYA ANGELOU

She worked hard. She worked smart. And finally, Alexandria landed a job, proudly calling it her first legitimate job ever. After nine jail stints and five unsuccessful attempts in rehab, that's no small accomplishment.

She works for an environmental services firm as a closed-circuit television (CCTV) operator. In her own apartment, she is now working to regain full custody of her son and to maintain a strong sober support network, including several *Saint John's* alums and members of a *Narcotics Anonymous* group.

During her time in jail, Alexandria met Natasha (not to be confused with Natisha) who remained a part of her support network. As Natasha witnessed her thrive at *Saint John's*, she grew inspired to follow her through the *Red Door* as well. Having grown up with a mother very similar to Alexandria's, Natasha also met with great success. As the two graduated side-by-side from *Saint John's,* they decided to become roommates, so they could continually encourage and support one another on the path to success.

Alexandria's fifteen graduating peers nominated her to provide the Valedictorian address. "Though raised by an addict and a criminal," Alexandria said, "I graduate tonight knowing I can do all of the things I need to do to provide for myself and my family – things I did not learn from my mom. If you want something different from your life…" she continued, the tears flowing, "I've learned you have to DO something different in your life. You must change."

Alexandria's Parole Officer attended graduation, too. She clapped wholeheartedly as Alexandria declared she was now fueled by love, hope, hard work, and happiness rather than chaos and pain.

— AUTHORS' OBSERVATION —

Face the Streets or Do the Time

Alexandria's story sparks an important public policy point. Many of the stories thus far revolve around two closely related worlds: the broken people who wind up homeless, and the broken people who enter the criminal justice system.

Noted earlier, approximately 60% of the women who enter the *Red Door* have criminal histories. But the parallels between the two populations run far deeper.

Taking a closer look at the issue demographics of the incarcerated and the homeless populations, both largely include people who grew up in poverty, struggle with mental illness, struggle with substance abuse, and lack a high school diploma or GED. Why, then, are our modern-day approaches to both populations so polar opposite when it comes to rehabilitation?

She is unstoppable, not because she has achieved perfection, not because she has it all figured out, not because she has overcome all of her doubts and fears. She is unstoppable because she has the strength and courage to continue.

As an example, through the mid-2000's, data available through the *California Department of Corrections and Rehabilitat*ion (CDCR) website featured a 66% recidivism rate – meaning two-thirds of those who entered prison returned there within three years of their release.

This high rate of return created many issues for the state, including prison overcrowding, which put added burden on the state's crowded prisons and the over-subscribed health care facilities. In 2006, the Federal Courts appointed a receiver to oversee health care in California's prisons.

To reduce prison overcrowding, CDCR's short-term changes included contracting with out of state and private prisons for bed space. In the longer term, they instituted a major policy shift called *Realignment* that included a focus on rehabilitation for those in prison and in addition, transferring lower level offenders to County jails.

Most relevant to this discussion, CDCR's new rehabilitative services included substance abuse education, mental health counseling, and GED classes. What's more, inmates received sentence reduction credits as an incentive to engage in services.

Guess what happened? According to the CDCR website, in just one decade, recidivism fell by over 20 percentage points.

On the other hand, *Housing First* takes the exact opposite approach. It completely divorced housing and services, ignoring the need for rehabilitation.

CDCR's rehabilitative approach led to fantastic results. In contrast, the non-rehabilitative approach of *Housing First* has had the exact opposite effect. Armed with this data, why do public policy makers ignore the need for rehabilitation? Good question.

Note: For additional information on California's Realignment plan and the reasons underlying it, visit www.cdcr.ca.gov/about-cdcr/strategicplan/.

Two Worlds Reflected in the Mirror

In 2016, CDCR approached *Saint John's* to spearhead a new program focused on successfully re-integrating women approaching the end of their sentences called the *Custody to Community Transitional Reentry Program* (CCTRP). CDCR inherently understood the direct correlation between the seemingly disparate incarcerated and homeless populations. At the time, some of *Saint John's* board members did not. As a result, the Board struggled with whether or not to adopt the program.

The Board eventually realized that, while *Saint John's* focused on ending a woman's homelessness, the program's underlying objective lay in bringing"real change" into an individual's life. Accordingly, this perspective allowed the Board to adopt the program.

Compared to the current recidivism rate for the general prison population (approximately 45%), CCTRP yielded an impressive recidivism rate of 6.5% in its first two years. (2020 Office of Research Data at CDCR). This kind of success is no accident and proves the program actually works. The significance and relevance regarding the homeless population is more than evident.

Alexandria's story, aside from the amazing success she achieved through her desire and effort, points to the misguided nature of our public policy response to these similar populations. Had Alexandria been released from jail directly to the streets, she is confident she would have returned to a life of crime. It is, after all, what her mom taught her, and all she knew herself.

So the question is: Would a place to live, in and of itself, have changed any of that? Absolutely not. Fortunately for Alexandria, she found a place to acquire the tools she needed to gain and maintain her sobriety, an apartment, and her family – to live out a productive life.

"The greatness of a community is most accurately measured by the compassionate actions of its members..."

CORRETTA SCOTT KING

CHAPTER 13

Growth of a Flower

Attempting new things, recognizing what does and does not work, and continually learning

She could do no wrong, it seemed. Proud of her zest, ambition, and all that she had accomplished at such a young age, Julianna's mom had such high hopes for her – and with good reason. A solid student, a great daughter, and a wild, infectious smile – Julianna was poised for a life of success.

At eighteen, just out of high school, she landed a fantastic job working in Operations for *Bally's Total Fitness*. Two solid years in, *Shape Health Clubs* snapped her up to run Club Acquisitions. Her career on the perfect trajectory, she also reveled in access to everything the health and fitness club had to offer. She invested long hours into the job, and on the gym floor as well. In more ways than one, Julianna became solid as a rock. Until the methamphetamines rudely interrupted and took her down.

A friend – someone she had met at the gym and whom she trusted – gave her some little pills along with the promise, "This stuff will take you to another level." Truer words were never spoken. The level, however, was downward, and the spiral immediate.

Julianna, a young, bright, shooting star, suddenly found herself starving for her next fix, ingesting, snorting, and doing whatever it took to get high. At first, it served as an excuse for working out, but that lasted only a little while before she was using to get by. She was always high. And as meth leads to more meth, she began hanging around others who were using as regularly as she – including a man who, after a one-night stand, became the father of her first son. The meth use carried on; he did not.

Soon thereafter, she met Curt. Their relationship was instantly wild and exciting, or so she convinced herself. Saturated in the toxic grip of meth, she ignored the violence, accepting it as part of "his way." But after their son was born, Curt beat her so badly that it attracted the attention of local authorities. CPS monitored her, watched her carefully, tested her regularly, and ultimately ensured her baby was safe.

He was anything but.

Julianna continued to use. She simply learned the tricks to creatively passing the drug tests. She gave birth to a second son by a different father. Born Tox Pos, CPS swiftly took the newborn baby and his brother into custody. Julianna's mother, thankfully, stepped in to "foster" the children, but in return, demanded she seek help.

Julianna entered a 90-day rehab program. Her mind somewhat clear, Julianna understood her struggle with addiction required more than a couple months of clean time. Her CPS worker (a former *Saint John's* employee) pointed her in the direction of the *Red Door*.

"For me, *Saint John's* was the last house on the block," Julianna says. "I knew I had to address the behaviors and the choices that got me there in the first place."

Getting sober was one small piece of Julianna's recovery. Beyond the self-improvement classes and the solid structure *Saint John's* provided, Julianna experienced a life-changing "'Aha!' moment" during a class discussion about the cycle of abuse.

"That's me!" she realized. "My boyfriend totally attacked me! He beat the crap out of me! Now he's in prison for it and still… still I am on his side?"

She suddenly realized his physical abuse was wrong – and criminal – and that she retained the choice of whether or not to end it.

Despite this major breakthrough, one of the harder things she faced at *Saint John's* was to watch other women reunify with their children. Julianna questioned whether she had screwed up "too badly." The clock ticking, CPS gave her nine months to get her act together and reach the benchmarks they set forth. Secretly, she wondered if all she put her kids through meant she could never be a good mother for her children.

But Julianna pressed on.

With the deadline looming over her head, she worked intensely on herself. Like working out in the gym when she was younger, she kept at it, checking off the CPS benchmarks one after the other. She attended every class available to her, including classes outside of *Saint John's*. She excelled in her employment training at *Plates*. Over and over, she stepped up for anything and everything extra that needed to be done. Through sweat and tears, she pushed herself like she had never pushed before. Knowledge, skills, confidence developed layer upon layer, like muscles on a bodybuilder; she grew stronger with each passing day, as the deadline steadily approached.

In the final weeks before her scheduled appointment with CPS, she landed a prized position as the General Manager of a Pilates studio. She then secured her own apartment. CPS noticed. Julianna fulfilled their many requirements. The only remaining question and her biggest fear was their question: "Can you provide for your boys as their mother, too?"

She responded confidently, "Yes. Yes, I can."

One week later, on August 7, 2018, like many she witnessed at *Saint John's*, Julianna reunited with her children, too.

Her resilient boys settled in quickly to their new routine, as did she. Her little family together again, she felt fulfilled and genuinely happy. Filled with gratitude and a confidence that she could help others in her shoes achieve it, too, she eventually began to offer support to other *Saint John's* clients and alums.

In September 2019, her employer made the decision to sell the Pilates studio. With her job at risk, she reached out to *Saint John's* for help, and ultimately gained a supervising position with *U.C. Davis*, where she now manages several fellow alumnae.

— AUTHORS' OBSERVATION —

The Commitment to Ongoing Growth

Julianna entered *Saint John's* feeling like a total failure. She doubted the very fiber of her being, including whether she could recover. Like a wilted flower, she stopped believing in the possibility that she would ever grow again.

In Julianna's corner were her family – her mom and her sister, who took custody and care of her boys during this period – and of course, her sons. Not only did they encourage and inspire her, she understood that her continued growth was the only way out, the only way to guarantee her future and theirs.

"I can no longer respond the way I used to..."

Sincerely, Growth

One of *Saint John's* core values, growth is not just a "nice" attribute, it's an absolute must-have value to permanently escape the cycle. The process begins with an open mind and an understanding that your past ways – both in thinking and in doing – led you to Saint John's. In order to never return to this state, you must change your thinking and your behavior – you must grow.

Saint John's honors and incentivizes growth, as it does with all of its core values. The more Julianna grew, the more rewards she earned, and in turn, the more she thrived. Momentum kicked in. The more she thrived, the more confidence she gained, and pretty soon, the Julianna of yesterday became unrecognizable. Her growth changed her life. Not only that: It saved her life.

CHAPTER 14

Generation Unto Generation

At 30 years old, Michelle B. finally got clean. Sick and tired, she drew a deep line in the sand, found real answers, and decisively broke the long-standing, generational cycle of addiction, poverty, and homelessness that had plagued her family for generations.

She was the fourth in her family to knock on the *Red Door.* Two years earlier, her cousin, Tamara, had knocked and entered. Aunt Diana followed. Then Mary, Michelle's mother. And finally, Michelle.

Cousins, Mary and Diana were raised primarily together by an Auntie in San Jose, California. They received adequate love, but very little parental guidance. Mary left the nest first. She married Carl, gave birth to a son, and four years later, to Michelle.

A veteran of the Vietnam War, Carl struggled with PTSD. His verbal abuse grew worse over time. By the time Michelle was just twelve years old, the effects of his wartime trauma had taken him over completely. He tried unsuccessfully to commit suicide, and for years moved in and out of psych wards.

Michelle turned to drugs – hard drugs, and meth in particular. She joined a gang. She dropped out of school.

With no high school diploma and few life skills, and after constant drinking and drug use, multiple crimes, revolving jail cell doors, too many abusive relationships, and four innocent children, life seemed to hold nothing for Michelle but more of the same. While holding her infant son, and with her five-year-old daughter clinging to the other arm, a drug-crazed boyfriend punched her in the face – the straw that finally broke the camel's back.

Both her cousin and her mother begged Michelle to consider *Saint John's*, where they found the support they needed to get back on track. If it worked for them, it might work for her as well. But given the limited "room at the inn," it wasn't just a matter of knocking on the door and waltzing in. Michelle called every day for over a month and a half.

The wait, while challenging on so many levels, made her want it even more. In early 2011, a space for her family finally opened up. "When I got that call," she says, "I remember saying to myself, 'Today is the day I start over! And I meant it.'"

Eighteen years into her addiction, Michelle immediately stopped using drugs – cold turkey. That's rare. She took full advantage of every resource and service *Saint John's* offered: substance abuse disorder classes, parenting, counseling, money matters, even the classes that sounded a little bit ridiculous to her, like "Positive Thinking."

She hated the sound of those words – positive thinking. "Whoever heard of something as stupid as that?"

But behind the *Red Door,* there was no wiggle room. She attended this "stupid class," and surprised herself by picking up new and interesting techniques. Today, she admits, "*Saint John's* turned my life around by teaching me to turn my thinking around."

She recalls when her class instructor (me) explained that, "When you are in a negative pattern of thought, even the 'most inconsequential' positive thought can move you out of it." Evidently, the instructor (me) used the example of simply looking over at someone else's shirt – whether it be the color, the style, the fit, or anything else – to find something positive to say about it and focus thinking there. For Michelle, it worked.

That day, Michelle realized that she was 100% in charge of, and responsible for, her thinking. For the first time in her life, she understood that when she became frustrated or angry, she retained the power and ability to control her response. She began to practice her new "trick" every day without fail.

"If I thought the way I used to think, my life would be in ruins today."

MICHELLE B.

During employment training at *Plates Cafe*, Michelle learned another "stupid" lesson: Time management. She recalls Chef Stu, then the head chef in the employment training program, drilling it into her head: Time management is a skill she would depend on for her success – in the kitchen, and especially as a single mother. Initially, she brushed him off. What did he possibly know about her life anyway? Now, realizing how fundamental it is to her success in her parenting, in her profession, and in her recovery, she laughs, "It's everything."

Initially, like so many clients, Michelle did not appreciate the value of the new skills she gained. She viewed the classes and these new techniques as "requirements" to live at *Saint John's*. She couldn't see it, but the ground began to shift under her feet. She sees it clearly now and recognizes that these "requirements" paved the way to her success and played a huge role in the way she raised her children.

While in a *Head Start* workshop, another class Michelle did not want to attend, she stumbled across another valuable lesson: The importance of showing up and being proactive. At the time, her son was too young for Head Start, but in an effort to "be proactive," she had placed his name on the waiting list anyway.

One year later, the enviable position of Head Chef on *Saint John's* primary campus opened up. Michelle was tapped to fill the role. Because her son was now enrolled in *Head Start*, Michelle could better manage the hours and was thus able to accept their offer.

With excitement and a tremendous sense of responsibility, she passionately prepared four meals each day for hundreds of women and children, providing guidance and inspiration as well. "Don't give up before the miracle happens," she'd advise them all. "Even when it seems too much to handle… be patient and keep your eye on the prize. I promise, good things will come!"

Words of wisdom.

During her tenure, Michelle met Matt, the man who would eventually become her husband. The single father of two children, he was enrolled in a vocational training program at one of *Saint John's* food suppliers. At first, Michelle didn't want anything to do with this man, despite his obvious interest in her. However, his genuine kindness and work ethic wore her down.

She soon accepted his affections and, eventually, his hand in marriage. In the fall of 2014, they relocated their family to Salem, Oregon, to be closer to Michelle's father and brother. Michelle's mother, Mary, decided to join them as well, as did Michelle's Aunt Diana. There, Michelle gained employment as a chef at a local hospital, while Matt took a job as a driver for *Sysco Foods*. Mother Mary and Aunt Diana cared for Matt and Michelle's six children.

One year later, Matt received an incredible offer as a journeyman bridge painter in Massachusetts. Off they went. Within one year of touching down, they purchased their first-ever home. An incredible moment for anyone, let alone someone once destined to be forever dependent, the entire family reveled in this achievement.

Once settled in their new home, Michelle felt ready for a new challenge. Watching her husband thrive, she pursued an apprenticeship in the same field – bridge painting. She eventually passed her final exam and advanced to full journeyman status by the end of the year – a credential held by very few women.

Their children are living the epitome of the American Dream. The oldest, Alexia (18), currently attends community college, with the goal of transferring to *Arizona State University* for a degree in Behavioral

Analysis. Gregory (17) is enrolled in a nearby residential program, part of his effort to address the trauma he faced while growing up with his dad. He is progressing well and spends weekends with the family. Faith (14) is a freshman at a prestigious vocational tech school, studying house carpentry. Josiah (14) attends the same school, though his focus is plumbing. Caden (12) and Sergio (9) are also doing well in school and are quite the accomplished wrestlers.

From the grip of a long, and generational cycle of abuse and homelessness to becoming productive members of society

When Michelle's mother made the decision to join them in Oregon, Michelle took the initiative to lay down a new law. In no uncertain terms, Michelle insisted that her mom change her child-rearing ways to match Michelle's newfound techniques if they were to live successfully under one roof. Through her education at *Saint John's*, Michelle realized that if her children were raised in the same way that she and her mom were – and if they thought and behaved accordingly – they would inevitably repeat the "old family cycle."

This might seem obvious to some, but without the new lessons Michelle learned while at *Saint John's*, including healthy boundary setting, communication, rules, and regulations, she would never have understood the need for insisting upon this change, nor would she have had the tools to communicate it to her mother. Yet that conversation, according to Michelle, made all of the difference in their success as a multi-generational family living under one roof.

"You cannot raise your children as your parents raised you... because your parents raised you in a world that no longer exists."

ALI BIN ABI TALIB

— AUTHORS' OBSERVATION —

Work Ethic Made the Difference

To say that I know Michelle and her family well is an understatement. Five of my nearly thirteen years at *Saint John's* were deeply intertwined with them, not including the many check-in moments we have all enjoyed since. If any story demonstrates the potentially formidable tentacles of the generational cycle, this family's story is it. And if one story proves that deep healing and lasting change are possible... their story is it.

Michelle and her family members were able to overcome their negative generational cycle because of the work ethic inherent in each one of them. In each case, it was buried deep inside, nowhere to be seen when they first walked through the *Red Door*.

Once Michelle found her footing at *Saint John's*, this work ethic literally oozed from her pores, as it did with her family members, too.

Each battled their own demons with vigor, working hard to move beyond their past and create a very different future. With every bite of success, each of them became hungrier for more.

Once she graduated from *Saint John's*, Michelle's cousin, Tamara, rose to chef and then head chef at a rehab center. Now she is a certified drug and alcohol counselor for this same facility. Michelle's Aunt Diana, having also maintained her sobriety and her newfound ways, lives with her daughter, Tamara, helping to raise her four children while she scales life's ladder.

Four incredible women and their ten combined children – each are doing well on their respective paths, paths that would have looked very different had they not stepped through the *Red Door*.

This extended family's example demonstrates how when women and children enter *Saint John's*, they "don't know what they don't know." Few, if any, have a vision beyond their dark past. It doesn't even appear dark to them – but it is all they have known up to this point.

I kept a box of straws on my desk to illustrate this point. When looking through a single straw, the perspective becomes very narrow. I drew upon this demonstration during that "stupid" positive thinking class, to explain how limited one's perspective is when viewing the world through the lens of the past.

What's more, human nature coerces them to turn down the new, since they have no idea how it will benefit them. With proper guidance and encouragement, they will begin to look forward and become open to personal growth.

Without it…

- **It's no wonder why many women don't initially opt for counseling. They have never experienced anything like it, and therefore don't understand its benefits.**

- **It's no wonder why women don't immediately respond to classes such as *Positive Thinking* or "How to enroll your child in Head Start" – because they have no concept what those things are.**

- **It's no wonder why women might not appreciate time management lessons, or similar self-improvement classes, because they have no context on how something so alien might benefit them.**

It is important to note that no woman comes to *Saint John's* under government or court mandate. Each woman finds her way through the *Red Door* freely, having drawn her line in the sand and made the decision for herself and her family. Through an initial orientation and vetting process, she gains a full understanding of the high barrier structure and the accompanying rules, and that those rules serve one function alone: to help her become independent and free. The barriers exist for the sake of effectiveness.

Each woman can exit the program whenever she chooses – and sadly, many do so before graduating.

The *Federal Department of Education* mandates high school students take biology, regardless of whether they show a propensity for it, or whether they show interest in the pursuit of a science-based vocation. Why isn't high school given its many mandates then considered too high barrier as well?

Without access to the *Red Door* and all they learned behind it, Michelle and her family say, unequivocally, that life would be far different – and far worse.

Helping people grow and realize their full potential should be society's measure of effectiveness, and the guidepost employed by government, and other funders, to make their investment decisions.

CHAPTER 15

The Greatest of These is Love

Imagine a tiny, baby bird. Then imagine placing a single, little pebble onto its back. Then another. And another. Each day, month after month, year after year, more and more pebbles get added. Left to fend for itself, now hopelessly pinned to the ground, this little bird cannot take flight – something all the other birds do so naturally. No parents or relatives to help. No friends to give it a "wing up." If you were this bird, where do you turn for help? How do you even begin to deal with this reality?

What, exactly, did Alicia do to deserve the cruel life into which she was born? Why did she endure such a world of pain from the very day she arrived on earth – a miserable life filled with drugs, hatred, violence, and abuse?

Nothing. Alicia did nothing to deserve any of it.

At just 9 years of age, her mom's boyfriend repeatedly molested Alicia. When he started on her younger sister, Alicia finally revealed the ugly truth to her older brother. He alerted his schoolteacher, who thankfully took it to the authorities. The damage, however, had already set in.

While the sexual abuse effectively ended, another type of abuse quickly replaced it. Alicia's mother, convinced that she had lied and concocted the whole charade to gain attention, completely turned her back on her. In a dire state of neglect and abuse, Child Protective Services (CPS) removed Alicia from her home. Suddenly, through no fault of her own, this little girl found herself thrust into a whole new chapter of disastrous foster care failures and a dark, bottomless pit of despair.

"It crushed me," Alicia now admits. "I don't remember laughing as a child. Ever. I felt completely broken inside. But what terrified me most," she says, "my horrible, recurring nightmares of the devil tying me up and laughing at me."

At thirteen years old, Alicia got pregnant. Abortion seemed the only viable solution. In the emotional darkness that followed, the system put her in a children's receiving home to await her next step. She waited – nothing.

Married and divorced twice by age 20, with two children, her daily diet now included alcohol and meth. She hid none of this, openly injecting herself as her small children looked on. Her third, drug-crazed husband got arrested and deported for severely beating her. Alicia again found herself alone, on the streets, this time with two children in tow.

Bad quickly led to worse, and her addictions grew even more severe. With no education, no work history or life skills, and now no place to call home, drugs became the only thing upon which she could depend. She wandered the streets during the day, sleeping in a variety of emergency shelters each night. For years this dark pattern continued, always ending with one more child. Unprotected, natural prey, she got pregnant once again, with child number nine – Mikhayla , nicknamed Memes. CPS stepped in immediately to remove the infant, so that all Alicia was able to give the little baby was a name.

Nine children, six abortions, one miscarriage, and two additional CPS cases later, her pain-filled life seemed unfathomably hopeless. No idea where to go or who to ask for help, she reached the end of her rope. Somehow, she found a Catholic church that gave her shelter one night and overheard someone mention a place called the "*Red Door*." Word on the street, however, warned that it was a really hard place to get into, and a really hard program. Harder than the way she was living then? She broke down, found a phone, and made the call.

By now an exhausted, weathered, 46-year-old woman, Alicia crossed over the *Saint John's* threshold with her 9-year-old daughter, Memes. Her first step in the right direction and one that turned her entire world around, she began building new tools to create a life she never dreamed possible.

She invested herself wholeheartedly, focusing initially on simple life skills, a basic but necessary foundation. She eagerly took advantage of counseling to address her past trauma – the same trauma she had unknowingly inflicted upon her own children. She jumped into parenting classes, high school diploma classes, and employment training. Through great struggle and determination, Alicia found and felt comforted by the unconditional love that surrounded her – the love for which she had longed for since she entered the world. She felt a new sense of strength and caught a glimpse of how she might, one day, stand confidently on her own two feet.

Saint John's structure and sobriety requirements – the ones shunned by HUD and Sacramento County – combined with the marked progress Alicia showed, served as the impetus for CPS to approve reunification with her teenage daughter, Hilary. A new family began to take root, and once stabilized, they all entered *Saint John's Independent Housing Program* together. After receiving her GED, Alicia came to realize that each new day was a gift, and that it's never too late.

Soon after Alicia's breakthrough, a serious setback hit her in the form of a *Hepatitis C* diagnosis. This unexpected curve ball put her job search plans on hold while she focused on rebuilding her health. No stranger to difficulty, with her new resolve and arsenal of tools, Alicia demonstrated a deep resilience and a raw determination as she faced this unexpected demon. Before, a stumbling block such as this would have thrown her right back into using drugs. Not this time.

Every woman is a unique being.
Any program committed to real help
must be individualized in that same way.

Saint John's adjusted the timeline of her program to enable Alicia to address the unanticipated health issues. As soon as she regained her health, and with a green light from her doctors, Alicia launched into her job search with a vengeance.

In March of 2014, Alicia landed a job in the back office of *Pick-N-Pull*, an auto dismantler. Hired by a man with no idea of her troubled past, she took that place by storm. Six years and four pay-raises later, Alicia remains part of the working fabric of *Pick-N-Pull*.

"I still amaze myself," she confesses with a grin. "I suit up and show up every day."

Nine years clean, sober, and strong, Alicia now pays her own rent, pays her taxes, and faithfully contributes to her 401(k). She enjoys strong relationships with all nine of her children, fifteen grandchildren, and one great grandchild. More importantly, she serves as a strong role model for all of them.

Alicia, finally free, is no longer tethered to a life that nearly destroyed her and her children. She built a new life that, given the way she grew up, she never could have fathomed. While she experiences the regular bumps and bruises that life imposes, Alicia broke the vicious cycle of pain and torment that nearly consumed her, her children, and her grandchildren.

— AUTHORS' OBSERVATION —

When the Going Gets Tough

Alicia was "that little bird with all the pebbles piled high on its back." Like so many others, Alicia entered the world heavily burdened and unable to find her way. But unlike many of those other birds, Alicia found the proper, individualized support that allowed her to finally realize her true potential.

Last, but certainly not least, the most obvious lesson to learn from Alicia? Real, sweeping change is possible, no matter your age. Not overnight, perhaps, and certainly not without hard work and significant effort, but 100% possible. Through a gradual, deliberate, and non-linear process, with a tailored, individualized program that required commitment, hard work, patience, and a whole lot of tough love from all those involved, Alicia spread her wings and flew.

CHAPTER 16

Lessons to be Learned

For nearly a decade, I taught a "positive thinking" class to the women of *Saint John's*. As one of the first classes required of our clients, it became almost like a foreign language course for many.

I would explain that every person is on a path to improve – a path to become the best versions of themselves – and that our lives are a continuum of improvement. Life is a continuum, where everything serves as a lesson for our continued growth.

As a continuum, then, naturally some people are further along in certain areas, yet further behind in others. My explanation aimed to open their eyes as to how hypocritical it is to judge another person who may appear to be behind in one area of life, even while ahead in another.

I always found it interesting how judgmental many of the women could be upon entering Saint John's. Perhaps raised in this way, or perhaps the only tool in their toolbox up to that point, they often, unknowingly, would insult a person in an attempt to feel better about themselves.

This way of viewing life is not, however, confined to those in positive thinking class. We all begin life with a great deal to learn. Hopefully, we learn our lessons along the way, acquire more and more tools, and through each experience, grow more knowledgeable and more harmonious with who we are called to be.

I view homelessness as a part of one's life continuum rather than a defining and permanent facet of their lives. The key lesson here, and where our current system fails so miserably, is that the point at which a person experiences homelessness should not be used to determine their future lot in life. The homeless should always be encouraged, incentivized, and expected to grow through and beyond it. However, today's policies lock the homeless in a veritable straitjacket.

Just as in life, growth looks different for each person, and takes place over different timeframes. Some will master certain aspects sooner, while others might need ongoing support to continue their progress.

From day shelters and tent cities to rehab facilities and high barrier programs such as *Saint John's*, many types of organizations can help grow beyond homelessness, working together to ensure a proper hand-off once individuals reach the next step on their path. Current policy does not see or delineate the unique lines and shapes of each puzzle piece. On the contrary, every piece is seen and treated identically and shoved in place, whether it fits or not.

"What you allow is what will continue."

BISHOP DALE BRONNER

LESSON 1: Encampments

In 2017, a very serious Hepatitis-A outbreak erupted within the homeless community of San Diego, California. Proliferating primarily through fecal contamination, illicit drug use, and the sharing of dirty needles, Hep-A spread like wildfire within the homeless community. Nearly 600 people became infected, 20 of whom lost their lives. Fifteen other states experienced subsequent outbreaks.

With the national attention this outbreak received, and the warnings from public health officials and physicians since, elected officials across the country should have had discussions on how to prevent these types of outbreaks, especially in homeless communities facing rampant spread.

San Diego's Hep-A example provided sufficient reason for local governments to consider exercising greater control over unregulated encampments. But its lesson went ignored, as many elected officials subsequently condoned, and even promoted, additional encampments with no regulations.

In 2019, *KOMO News* reported that Seattle City Councilwoman Kshama Sawant sponsored legislation to create 40 new encampments across the city, despite the outcomes of a nearby encampment, Licton Springs, which had led to chaos and a 220% crime increase, and despite the warnings out of San Diego.

Mayor Libby Schaaf of Oakland, California also promoted unregulated encampments, again despite the lesson from San Diego. (Mayor Schaaf finally reversed her position in 2019, citing the frequent violence and "out of control" fires that threatened the people living in the encampments and the surrounding community.)

Often called tent cities, these unregulated encampments lack hygiene, sanitation, and any sort of abiding law, unless or until a resident or group of residents decide to exercise their own form of authority. *The National Law Center on Homelessness & Poverty*, a legal organization dedicated to ending homelessness, reports that homeless encampments have risen by 1,342% in the last decade alone.

"If we keep doing what we're doing, we're going to keep getting what we're getting.""

STEVEN COVEY

I do not discount the need or value of homeless encampments. On the contrary, I am a firm believer that regulated encampments should be part of the new homelessness continuum – as long as they are regulated and focus on supporting the homeless to progress and grow. (*Pinellas Hope*, discussed later in the book, provides a fantastic example.) Elected officials must address the issue of encampments to protect public health and public good.

LESSON 2: A Public Health Crisis

America was largely caught off-guard by the COVID-19 pandemic. The old adage "acting before thinking often leads to regret" was put into practice as a result.

As it relates to the homeless, had we heeded the lessons out of San Diego's Hep-A outbreak, we likely would have tackled, or perhaps still be in the midst of discussions, as to how to best serve both the sheltered and unsheltered AND the general public during a public health emergency.

For instance, which type of shelters would best control the spread of disease? Some shelters feature large rooms with a number of beds, according to the building's capacity. Other shelters provide bedrooms that might limit capacity but might also limit the spread of disease.

As an example, *Saint John's* operates three types of residential facilities: one houses two families per bedroom, or up to four individual women per bedroom; one offers each family their own room; and yet another facility provides women without children a room with three to five roommates. These facilities all operate under the same strict cleanliness guidelines, but they are quite different in design. Is one better than the other, and for which segment of the homeless population in terms of preventing disease spread?

Motel rooms were tapped as temporary shelter from the pandemic. This seemed to be a win-win-win: at least for the homeless, for government, and for the motel owner who desperately needed revenue.

But with no time for deliberation, there was little discussion as to who gets sent to a potentially crowded shelter and who gets sent to a nice motel room that offers privacy and freedoms that a shelter may not. (And per the upcoming Lesson 3, do the homeless get to choose? Can they leave the motel room or shelter given the pandemic? How are the rules enforced?)

Another important, and largely ignored, consideration: Once the pandemic ends, what will happen to the homeless temporarily housed in motels? Do we simply toss them back out onto the street? Who will make these decisions – and are they even legal?

The pandemic hit so hard and so fast, communities had no time to deliberate these questions. Having learned nothing from our past, we were caught with our proverbial pants around our ankles.

Obviously, we cannot turn back the clock to the time of the San Diego outbreak, but we can, and must, demand that, post-pandemic, our elected officials learn something valuable from it – and that the solutions arising from it be based on continued growth and effectiveness.

THE CARES ACT

— $4B tranche of funding for the homeless —
HUD authorized the following:
(HUD.gov 2020)

• ***Build more emergency shelters for homeless individuals and families.***

• ***Operate emergency shelters by providing maintenance, rent, repair, security, fuel, equipment, insurance, utilities, food, furnishings, and supplies necessary for the operation.***

• ***Provide hotel/motel vouchers for homeless families or individuals.***

• ***Provide the essential services to people experiencing homelessness, including child care, education services, outreach, employment assistance, outpatient health services, legal services, mental health services, substance abuse treatment services, and transportation.***

• ***Prevent individuals from becoming homeless, and rapidly rehouse homeless individuals.***

HUD authorized all this new funding under *Housing First,* meaning that basic, seemingly crucial practices – required temperature testing upon entry or the requirement of face masks – will not be allowed for non-profits that accept this funding. That would be considered too high barrier.

Not only does this conflict with the Center for Disease Control (CDC's) best practices for COVID-19 prevention, it is not in the best interest of the homeless, nor the people who staff the non-profits serving them, nor the public health in general.

LESSON 3: Personal Choice

Another important lesson to consider relates directly to the homeless and personal choice. For instance, during the 2020 pandemic, many documented cases arose around the homeless declining the offer of shelter, or choosing to leave the shelter they were provided prior to the pandemic's conclusion.

California acquired 16,400 motel rooms in a $150 million effort to house roughly 90,000 unsheltered people during the pandemic. Yet as of September 2020, at one point, only 11,700 of the hotel rooms were actually occupied as recorded in the September 2020 *CalMatters* tracker (www.calmatters.org). According to this same tracker, in Los Angeles County, more than a third of the roughly 6,600 people who moved into motel rooms left prematurely – because they wanted to.

As discussed earlier in the book, many of the homeless struggle with *Anosognosia* (a deficit of self-awareness) due to their addiction. Others have stated they do not "want" to abide by the structure and rules under which even the lowest barrier shelters operate. Some are overtly suspicious of anything government has to offer.

What happens if they don't like the options offered, or if they simply prefer to stay on the streets? Do they maintain a personal choice in these matters? If the answer is no – on behalf of the greater good – elected officials then need to decide how to best enforce it.

If the answer is yes, then these same officials have another challenging discussion ahead – answering why the general public must obey rules from which the homeless are exempt. When and why is it acceptable for the general public to be "forced" to live under government mandates – such as social distancing and wearing masks – while the homeless get to choose whether to do so or not? How can the government mandate the immediate closure of a thriving, tax-paying business, but not enforce any regulations on the homeless?

On April 17th, 2020, *CBS Austin* reported that several members of the community had raised this very question. Evidently, the public mandate issued by Austin Mayor Steve Adler and Travis County Judge Sarah Eckhardt exempted the homeless from the public requirement to wear a face mask. All other Austinites faced a Class-B Misdemeanor citation for breaking the same rule. In fact, according to the City of Austin and the Travis County websites, the homeless are exempted from nearly every public health guideline that applies to everyone else living there.

During this pandemic, for many taxpayers and business owners, the freedom of personal choice went right out the window. Restaurants didn't get to decide whether or not to remain open based on the way they were feeling. People didn't shelter in place because it was a good excuse to stay home from work.

This is indeed a complex issue. But our elected leaders should consider these examples as they formulate policy post-pandemic. We have the responsibility to ensure they do so.

LESSON 4: Effectiveness of Policies

I've already spent a good deal of time pointing out the issues with *Housing First* – applied as a one-size-fits-all approach – and the false assumption that "a roof over their head" is all the homeless need. Placing all the blame on *Housing First*, however, isn't entirely accurate either. Another offender also plays a role: *Harm Reduction*.

Originating in the United Kingdom in the late 1980s as an approach to control disease within the drug-using population, *Harm Reduction* seeks to reduce the negative effects associated with the use of drugs. In other words, an individual can choose to use illegal substances, and providers should mitigate the effects of them doing so. In the United States, largely over the period of 2012-2016, *Harm Reduction* principles were then embraced and embedded at the federal and local levels.

Under this approach, cities such as Los Angeles, New York, Chicago, Philadelphia, and San Francisco instituted needle exchange programs, and proposed safe injection sites for those using drugs such as heroin.

It should go without saying that heroin is illegal for good reason. According to the *National Institute of Health* (NIH), heroin overdoses kill over 15,000 Americans annually – roughly the same number who die from brain cancer. It's worth taking a closer look at this policy and how it relates to homelessness in particular.

Given that 75% of the homeless struggle with drug and alcohol addiction, we are actually facilitating the ability of those living in the aforementioned cities to engage in ongoing, illegal drug use.

Earlier I cited a *USA Today* analysis showing that 48 of the 50 of the top U.S. cities have experienced a marked spike in homelessness over the last several years. Many of these cities also operate under both the *Housing First* and *Harm Reduction* policies. The City of Los Angeles provides a great example as to how these same policies have trickled down, undermining both the homeless and the public good.

Fire Station 9, covering LA's notorious *Skid Row*, was recognized as the busiest firehouse in America. In 2019, in just one year, the station responded to 35,518 calls for service, according to the Los Angeles Fire Department, including a record high number of overdose and mental-health emergencies.

In 2006, however, *Fire Station 9's* phone rang a mere 6,654 times according to Los Angeles' KCET. Back then, L.A. Police Chief Bill Bratton and LAPD Central Division Commander Andrew Smith implemented an abstinence-based pilot program for the policing of *Skid Row* called "The Safer Cities Initiative" in which strict rules were established and enforced. Interested in effectiveness first, these individuals considered the problem through an alternative lens.

According to a study done by Gary Blasi and the UCLA School of Law, their approach led to an impressive 45% reduction in violent crime throughout the jurisdiction (a 39% reduction inside *Skid Row)*, a 50% reduction in overdose deaths, and a 75% reduction in homicides. The overall homeless population during this period also declined from 1,876 people to just 700.

Under increasing pressure from civil rights lawsuits and public pressure campaigns, however, elected officials began to systematically dismantle the initiative, due to concerns that it "criminalized" homelessness. With no real or effective counterforce to these groups, the Safer Cities Initiative was abandoned within a decade.

Since that time, the homeless population on *Skid Row* has again skyrocketed – from 700 to nearly 4,800 people and rising, according to Los Angeles' latest Point in Time (PIT) count. In L.A.'s Central Division alone, crime increased by 59% since 2010, with officers responding to 13,122 incidents in 2019.

Former homeless addict Richard Copley, now working with the Midnight Mission, confesses that while on Skid Row and in the depths of his meth addiction, that he had a motel room thanks to the government, but preferred to spend the night in his street-side tent to be "closer to the action."

Estimates are that many of *Skid Row's* poor, addicted, disabled, and mentally ill residents are already housed in its dense network of permanent supportive-housing units, emergency shelters, Section 8 apartments, and single-room-occupancy hotels. However, many of their friends remain on the streets, as does "the action." Under *Harm Reduction*, they "safely" use on these streets, and under *Housing First*, they "use" in the safety of their own place. No wonder they don't aspire to more. No wonder they have stopped growing.

Please understand – I am not saying that *Housing First* or *Harm Reduction* were the sole cause(s) for the spike. I would, however, point out the ground level data that resulted from the disbanding of the *Safer Cities* initiative, and while *Housing First* and *Harm Reduction* kicked in. If numbers don't lie, then something clearly went horribly wrong. What did we learn?

LESSON 5: Personal Growth

The question of an individual's right to "do as they please," particularly regarding the use of illegal drugs, presents another huge concern and lesson to be learned. It cannot simply be a matter of right and wrong, or ethics alone. While ethics certainly play a role in the matter, another perspective might ask whether people are getting better – or worse.

With personal growth as a lens, let's look once more at the approach of *Harm Reduction*.

One of L.A.'s most high-profile, non-profit organizations (to remain nameless) – not a shelter but a provider of "services" to the homeless – celebrated their provision of "clean needles" to more than 12,000 addicts in 2019. If that is the sole definition of success, then we should all applaud.

But, before we do that, let's add personal growth to our success barometer first.

Of those who received the 12,000 clean needles, less than 1% then took advantage of any further services offered by the non-profit, including the opportunity to enroll in this same organization's free outpatient drug-treatment program. That doesn't sound like forward movement, and at what cost to the taxpayer?

According to this organization's 2017 audited financial statements, 84% of its $6 million operating budget came from government sources – i.e., taxpayers. If the argument is whether or not an individual has the right to choose to use an illegal drug, what then, is the choice of the taxpayer, who inevitably becomes saddled with the ongoing tab?

Evidence reveals that an individual under the steady influence of drugs presents far greater costs to public health and public safety systems. And they present an even greater risk to others and the public good.

In 2013, according to *Adam II* data collected by the *National Institute of Corrections* (NIC), between 63% and 83% of those who committed crimes – including harm to individuals or businesses – tested positive for drugs. Among those charged with property crimes, 56% reported being under the influence of drugs at the time of the crime. These data suggest a high correlation between drug use and crime, resulting in the risk of a significant impact to society.

In avoiding harm for the addict, we then endanger the general public, while demanding that the public continue to foot the bill. Everything we do, every policy we enact, every tax dollar spent, must be weighed and measured through the filter of growth and overall effectiveness.

Is handing a drug addict a clean needle helpful? Yes, in some ways it is. But does it improve the life of that individual as well as the whole of society? If it doesn't, therein lies the opportunity for a lesson learned as to how that might be adjusted or changed to do so. Our elected officials need to ask and answer these questions, and we all need to learn from them.

LESSON 6: Requiring Treatment

The National Institute of Health (NIH) defines addiction as, "...a form of mental illness: a complex brain disorder characterized by continued and compulsive drug use despite harmful consequences and long-lasting changes to the brain..."

It is classified as a disease.

Given the majority of addicts suffer from *Anosognosia* (an inability to know they're ill), and given the ongoing harm to the brain, are we, as a society, negligent under *Housing First* and *Harm Reduction* policy? Are we, in a sense, liable for malpractice?

Stay with me here…

American hospitals are required, by law, to provide necessary emergency medical treatment to anyone who walks through their door, regardless of insurance. We all learned during the COVID-19 pandemic that a hospital is not necessarily just a tall building on the corner of Main Street with four white walls, medical supplies, and beds. A hospital can quickly become any place you need it. During the height of the pandemic, for example, New York City saw Central Park quickly converted into a temporary hospital, was along with a convention center, and even a U.S. Navy hospital ship that provided additional capacity.

If this is true, then why not turn our public street corners into hospital units, to meet people right where they are in an effort to treat their mental illness?

Homelessness is a national crisis, and mental illness, including addiction, largely underlies it. Are we morally negligent in not treating addiction, by enacting policies that discourage non-profits from trying? Further, what does our failure mean to taxpayers who underwrite the costs required to sustain the homeless – to feed them, to provide their healthcare, to provide their income – for the rest of their lives, with no expectation of recovery or reasonable management of their condition?

Keep in mind that according to the *Urban Institute*, approximately 75% of the homeless are unemployed – they rely on public subsidies such as welfare assistance, and/or illegal means, to sustain their drug habit. They are more likely to use the public health system for their ongoing health needs and are more likely to be involved with the criminal justice system, all underwritten by the American taxpayer.

Even if employed, there are "shared costs" to addiction. According to the *National Council on Alcoholism and Drug Dependence* (NCADD), American employers spend $81 billion (with a B) each year on addiction-related issues, including lost productivity, absenteeism, and health care costs. These expenses are not absorbed by the companies but are passed along to customers and/or the general public in the form of higher prices.

Taxpayers pay for it coming and going.

Also to be considered are the very real opportunity costs. If *Skid Row* was not inhabited by the homeless, what kind of vital economic output could this prime Los Angeles real estate generate? What's more, if those addicted and unemployed stopped using drugs, and became even slightly more productive, how much more would the public benefit from their actions?

Today, we must consider both as lessons – providing treatment and not providing treatment.

"I have spent many years of my life in opposition, and I rather like the role."

ELEANOR ROOSEVELT

1. Alexandria and family
2. Alicia and family
3. Alexandria at work
4. Alicia and family
5. Julianna and sons
6. Julianna and son
7. Sheila's graduation

8. Olliver - Inspirational Studies class
9. Olliver and granddaughter Victoria
10. Sheri and her son's family
11. Sheri, her daughter and boyfriend
12. Mandy and family
13. Mandy's hilarious kids
14. Sheila and family

15. Mary, Dina, Tamara and Michelle B. - 4 generations!
16. Michelle B's wrestling champs
17. Natisha, husband and children
18. Natisha - remote learning with daughter
19. Adrianna at work
20. Jennifer and her son
21. Jennifer speaking at Saint John's event

CHAPTER 17

The Unsung Heroes

As I have mentioned often, there is no such thing as a one-size-fits-all solution to homelessness. Under ubiquitous implementation of *Housing First* and the promise that it would "end homelessness," many non-profit organizations considered high barrier closed their doors due to the loss of funding and their inability to obtain replacement funding in time.

The non-profits that chose to follow the federal government's directive in order to survive – not necessarily because they believed it was right – were virtually the only ones left standing.

Thankfully, a handful of outstanding high barrier programs remained open because they had, at some point in their history, made the decision to diversify their revenue rather than relying solely on government contracts. Also key to their survival: They had established, effective fundraising teams that could quickly fill the revenue void left by government's shift to low barrier only. These dark periods included layoffs, service cutbacks, and many sleepless nights on the part of entire organizations.

Few enjoy opposition for the sake of opposition. But due to their deep commitment to helping people – truly helping them, rather than just giving them a temporary place to sleep – this group of non-profits found themselves swimming against the government-led tide in their communities. By not towing the party line, they were considered "the opposition." So be it.

But now more than ever, these programs – several introduced below – need your encouragement, your time, and especially your financial support. They, like *Saint John's*, should be considered for nationwide replication.

HOMESTRETCH

Fairfax, Virginia • *homestretchva.org*

Homestretch addresses the root causes of homelessness for each family, helping them overcome their underlying issues. Their clients arrive on their doorstep in complete despair, many fleeing for their lives from domestic abuse. Almost all are trapped in a cycle of poverty.

One of few programs like it in the country, *Homestretch* provides comprehensive services to gather each family, address each barrier, and enable permanent change. Their families can achieve transformational change because *Homestretch* addresses every problem in their lives with sufficient support to make swift and lasting progress.

Because they maintain high expectations are high, have faith in the capabilities of their families, and remove all the reasons "why they can't," *Homestretch* families make greater and more fundamental changes in their lives than they ever thought possible.

In 2016, due to their "requirements" of families, *Homestretch* lost approximately $600,000 in annual funding, crucial operating funds that had fueled their organization for dozens of years. The withdrawal of this funding had nothing to do with their actual outcomes. Rather, they lost funding because they refused to "toe the government line." Thankfully, due to an extraordinary fund-raising effort, the community has filled the substantial void left in the manifest miscalculation of a *Housing-First*-only approach.

MARIAN HOUSE

Bethesda, Maryland • *marianhouse.org*

A transitional housing and intensive rehabilitation program for homeless women and their children, *Marian House I* – their entry level program – serves 14-18 families at any given time. They provide intensive supportive services, including education, employment, and counseling during this phase.

Once families achieve their initial goals, they can move on to *Marian House II*, where they live in a community setting along with others striving to achieve similar goals for healthy living. Families continue to receive supportive services as they pursue their larger rehabilitation goals in a more independent setting.

In 2016, due to the high barrier requirements of the families they serve, they lost $400,000 in annual funding which – as of the writing of this book – totals over $1.4 million lost to date. Thankfully, due to an extraordinary fund-raising effort on their part, the local community stepped up to fill the gap so *Marian House* could continue their amazing work.

The language used here sounds similar to the loss described with *Homestretch.* It is intentionally cookie-cutter to make a point that these losses were not due to outcomes but to existing and necessary requirements that were suddenly considered high barrier.

SOLUTIONS FOR CHANGE

San Diego, California • *solutionsforchange.org*

Founded in 1999 by social entrepreneurs Chris and Tammy Megison, *Solutions for Change* was born based on a harsh reality: "It just isn't right for a baby to sleep on the floor of a winter emergency shelter."

The Megisons' model, now known as *Solutions University*, blends affordable housing, educational opportunities, employment training, and other health related solutions, all within a cohesive, strategic partnership. Their efforts center on one goal: work with their community to permanently solve family homelessness for kids and the communities.

In 2016, due to the high barrier requirements of the families they serve, they lost a whopping $600,000 in annual funding, totaling nearly $2 million as of 2020. Yet again, this had nothing to do with their incredible outcomes. Rather, they lost funding, as you might suspect, because they refused to bend their knee to the king: *Housing First.*

Thankfully, due to an extraordinary fund-raising effort on their part, the local community filled the financial gap so *Solutions* could continue to fulfill its mission. The *Solutions* model should be praised, supported, and duplicated, not neglected by government authorities, as under the *Housing First* approach.

Once again, as with *Homestretch* and *Marion House*, the language used here begins to sound redundant. And it is, making the point that these losses were not due to outcomes but to existing and necessary requirements that were suddenly considered high barrier.

COMMUNITY FIRST! VILLAGE

Austin, Texas – *mlf.org*

A development of *Mobile Loaves & Fishes*, *Community First! Village* is a 51-acre, master-planned community that provides affordable, permanent housing for over 200 formerly homeless men and women.

Everyone pays rent that ranges from $225 to $430 per month, making each person carry their own weight. Many *Community First!* residents are employed by the various on-site enterprises, including a farm, a woodworking shop, and an outdoor movie theater. Beyond 200 full-time residents, their little town also hosts volunteers from church groups, art class students, even tourists welcomed as *AirBnB* guests in an assortment of stylishly designed "tiny homes" in an effort to bring more people into regular contact and conversation with the homeless.

Maintenance of these shared spaces also provides a source of employment for residents. Earning anywhere from $350 to $900 a month, they clean the kitchens and bathrooms, and contribute to the general upkeep of the village itself. Community residents earned nearly a million dollars of "dignified income" in 2017 and 2018.

This model works for so many reasons, including the focus on each individual's participation and growth, and of course, the therapeutic community aspect of the program – in both name and design. *Community First!* truly lives a "people first" model.

Community First! leadership made an early decision to avoid government funding given its *Housing First* strings. While they did not lose money in government's pendulum shift to *Housing First*, they could do so much more of the "good" described above with additional resources.

DELANCEY STREET

San Francisco, CA • *delanceystreetfoundation.org*

A residential, self-help organization for former substance abusers, ex-convicts, homeless, and others who have hit rock bottom, *Delancey Street* started in 1971 with just four people in a tiny San Francisco apartment. Serving thousands of residents today in five locations throughout the United States, residents range from teenagers to senior citizens, both men and women, of all races and ethnicities. Most struggle with hard-core drug and alcohol addiction, have served time in prison, are unskilled and/or functionally illiterate, have a personal history of violence, and suffer from generations of poverty.

Residents stay at *Delancey Street* for at least two years. Most remain for up to four years – all drug, alcohol, and crime free. During their stay, residents receive a high school equivalency degree (GED) and receive training in three different, marketable skills. Beyond academic and vocational training, residents also learn important values and the social and interpersonal skills to live successfully in mainstream society.

Any act of violence, or threat of violence, becomes cause for immediate removal. Interestingly, former gang members, many of whom have sworn to kill each other, live and work peacefully, side-by-side. Residents learn to grow together, promoting non-violence through a principle they call "each-one-teach-one," in which the "older" residents take responsibility, not just for their own personal growth, but also as mentors for new clients.

Interesting side note: *Saint John's*, when considering the launch of its first social enterprise – *Plates Café and Catering* – sent several staff members including myself and our lead volunteer for the project to *Delancey Street* for an intensive, two-day training session. We have sent several staff and board members since. We also incorporated many of the *Delancey Street* principles, including "each-one-teach-one" into *Saint John's*, and those principles remain in place today.

HAVEN FOR HOPE

San Antonio, Texas • *havenforhope.org*

Haven for Hope offers a place of new beginnings. They coordinate and deliver an efficient system of care for those experiencing homelessness. Not only do they provide the necessities of food, clothing, and shelter, but their larger effort, and the foundation on which they stand, provides long-term solutions that address the root causes of homelessness.

In order to address the individual needs of people, *Haven For Hope* collaborates with more than 140 partner organizations to provide over 300 comprehensive services, such as housing support, income development, employment training, education, counseling, life skills, legal services, child care, and many other services on a 22 acre campus. Serving more than 1,700 people, including 300 children, every day, clients receive the tools to move from homelessness to self-sufficiency and independent living.

This model focuses on individual growth, and embodies the homeless continuum for which I strongly advocate. Virtually everything the homeless need is there in one place. Their contained continuum makes it significantly less likely that people – and the issues that plague them – fall through the cracks. The integrated service model facilitates communication: mental health counselors more easily coordinate with addiction counselors, who then coordinate with employment training coordinators, child care coordinators, and more – all of whom see the client from different but uniquely helpful perspectives.

PINELLAS HOPE

Clearwater, Florida • *pinellashope.org*

Pinellas Hope was established in December 2007 on a 10-acre plot of land through a unique partnership with

Catholic Charities, the interfaith community, local government, businesses, and other not-for-profit organizations. They serve homeless adults living on the streets by providing them with 250 temporary, emergency shelter beds in tents.

Over the years, they expanded to include the *Pinellas Hope II*, which boasts a community center, permanent administrative offices, a kitchen, library, computer room, pavilion/covered dining area, men's and women's bathrooms, showers, a laundry room, and more than 150 efficiency apartments that provide supportive housing to residents, in preparation for a return to regular housing.

Residents receive assistance with food, transportation, employment, and numerous wrap-around social services – including medical and dental, eye exams, adult education/GED classes, mental health, and many more – as they work towards a return to self-sufficiency.

This model is growth-focused and provides a therapeutic community for the most chronically homeless, primarily those coming directly from the streets. Pinellas meets them right where they are, and at the same time, recognizes the place at which they entered. Pinellas need not define them going forward; instead, the clients shepherd themselves to a life previously unimaginable.

CITYGATE NETWORK

North America • *citygatenetwork.org*

Citygate Network is North America's oldest and largest community of independent, faith-based crisis shelters and life-transformation centers. In most U.S. cities, a member of the *Citygate Network* provides the most comprehensive homeless services available; in some cities, it is the only homeless services provider.

Through the process of a gospel-powered life transformation, the 300 organizations in the network seek to move people in desperate situations and destitute conditions to a place where they can flourish.

The breadth-of-life transformation work can be described with their eight "S" values:

- **Saved:** making choices that will keep them from chronic illness and physical death;
- **Sober:** no longer controlled by stimulants or depressants;
- **Stable:** mentally and emotionally balanced and enjoying good health;
- **Schooled:** enriched with the fundamental knowledge to be competent and competitive;
- **Skilled:** being academically credentialed and set on a career path;
- **Secure:** able to provide financially for themselves and their loved ones;
- **Settled:** benefitting from having the same safe place of their own to stay every night;
- **Serving:** giving back to the community through missional living.

Citygate's "S" model is spot on. It seamlessly threads its 300 members together. There is no one-size-fits-all under *Citygate*. Combined, its members model the new continuum proposed throughout this book.

PRIDE INDUSTRIES

Roseville, California • *prideindustries.com*

I adore both what *PRIDE Industries* stands for and its longtime leader, Mike Ziegler.

Mike joined *PRIDE* in 1983, transforming a small church basement organization from an organization with 65 employees and a tiny $250,000 annual operating budget into a full-fledged manufacturing and service company employing 5,600 full-time staff, and with over $340 million in annual revenue. Today, *PRIDE* is among America's largest non-profit employers of people with disabilities.

Mike was the driving force behind PRIDE's incredible success. Not only was he a fantastic, charismatic, hard-driving, tireless leader, not only did he pave the way toward the organization's incredible transformation and growth, Mike also deeply loved, and believed in, each individual *PRIDE* serves.

Day in and day out, *PRIDE* proves that "everyone can work," and that by helping them do so, we unleash their full human potential. As you walk through their main facility, a vast range of people struggling with mental and physical disabilities – from mildly disabled to clearly visible quadriplegics – are working. Everyone is happy and productive. It is a "people first" model that should expand policy makers' vision for solving homelessness, and the power of helping people do for themselves. In parallel with the individuals they serve, they grew out of their mistakes and their successes. By no means have any achieved perfection, but they continue to grow toward their full potential.

In late 2019, Mike was diagnosed with Stage Four cancer. Unfortunately, Mike recently lost this battle. I pray for his family and the PRIDE, family that they continue his incredible legacy.

All of these program models, including *Saint John's*, started as small, struggling, entrepreneurial efforts. As they grew, they undoubtedly stumbled – and refined. As they perfected their models, and as their models became proven, they expanded based on one thing alone – their results – helping people obtain and maintain real change in their lives.

In combination, these organizations give shape to the new homelessness continuum I reference often in the book.

"If the ladder is not leaning against the right wall, every step we take just gets us to the wrong place faster."

STEVEN COVEY

CHAPTER 18

The Open Door

Taking the Necessary Next Steps

Homelessness is so huge and complex that it leaves many with the feeling it is an insurmountable problem. In solving this crisis, we must look to take one bite of the elephant at a time.

Indeed, employing this same attitude can help an individual overcome the myriad issues necessary to overcome their homelessness. As discussed in Chapter 2 – *The Red Door*, when an individual first enters the program, the team purposefully focuses her on the first step – the first bite versus the vast number of bites necessary to achieve self-sustainability. The next step is a bit easier, and the next even easier. Pretty soon, momentum kicks in which furthers progress.

But it all begins with one step: the first step.

In early 2016, I pulled into the parking lot of *St. John's Lutheran Church* – my family's church for many years, and the birth parent of *Saint John's.* As I tried to find a parking place, I encountered a throng of people lining up for Winter Sanctuary – a migrating winter shelter the church was hosting that week. One man, smoking a cigarette, tossed it to the ground directly in front of my car. He didn't do it to harass me; it was more of a carefree, habitual motion. He barely noticed the cigarette was still lit.

As it became clear that he did not intend to either extinguish or dispose of it, I rolled down the window, pointed to the ground, and asked, "Is that your cigarette?" I can still see the dumfounded look on his face. A bit taken aback, he responded affirmatively, "Yeah...." I pressed him, asking who he thought would pick it up. He didn't have an answer. "Do you want me to pick it up?" he asked. "Yes, I do," I responded. "Please extinguish it first, then throw it in the trash."

He did.

This man did not get angry, upset, or even roll his eyes at me. He simply followed through on my request.

What struck me as odd in this exchange? This man was being offered safe refuge at our church for one full week, meals included, at no cost to him – a clean and loving environment where he would be treated with kindness and respect by church volunteers. Given his innocent reaction to the cigarette incident, he did not recognize he had done anything wrong, nor that he had a responsibility to clean up after himself. Neither did he comprehend the concept of "keeping safe" the very place that was attempting to keep him safe.

In this moment, I realized that "We, the People" are in really big trouble. For the first time, I saw it clearly: The *Housing First* and *Harm Reduction* policies our country had put in place over the last decade to "help the homeless" had actually done the opposite.

"We encourage what we tolerate."

UNKNOWN

In this particular man's case, these policies had essentially trained him – and so many others – to leave trash for others to pick up, to defecate on public sidewalks without regard for others who use those same sidewalks, and to toss dirty needles onto our streets for someone else to deal with, thereby placing that someone at risk of infection.

We have completely disconnected those experiencing homelessness from one of the most simple, yet important, realities in life. Along with individual rights comes a responsibility to take care of oneself, and to leave this world a better place – or at least to try to do so. It is not a stretch to suggest that society cannot function without these two truths working hand-in-hand.

Our streets are filled with fallout from "no skin in the game" policies – providing that people will be taken care of forever, whether they lift a finger to help themselves or not.

As Steven Covey so aptly stated, "Our ladder is leaning against the wrong wall." It's time to move the ladder to the right wall and start climbing out of this mess that we have created.

The homelessness system must provide a growth-focused continuum that supports people to progress. It will not work any other way.

Human beings are challenged throughout life to grow and improve to progress to the next level: from preschool through elementary school, through high school and college; from our daily household chores assigned at age five to our more advanced responsibilities as teenagers; from our place in the Daisy/Cub Scout troop to our role in the Girl or Eagle Scouts; from the car seat to the driver seat; from the entry level job to the first big promotion.

To thrive as human beings, people need to invest effort to grow and improve themselves. Though this effort looks different for each individual, the homelessness continuum should mirror what life so profoundly embodies: To live is to grow.

I think about it this way…

In 2013, my husband Jim suffered a massive heart attack, called the "widow-maker." Thank God, Jim was among the 5% who survived. But the attack so weakened his heart that in 2014, he received a heart transplant.

Every intervention, or non-intervention, in life comes with a cost. The cost of Jim's transplant – borne mostly by our insurance provider – came to just under $2 million, including his immediate pre and post-care. But this price tag did not include the 10 months of care leading up to the transplant, nor the ongoing care required after his transplant, nor the many drugs he requires to survive today to ensure his heart continues to function well. This analogy is not, however, a story about a heart attack or transplant, or even the survival of it. It's a story of recovery – and the continued personal growth that results from it – when we choose to invest in it.

Within two months after his transplant, Jim returned to work. He led the successful merger of the company he was running as president – an employer of about 120 people. The merger resulted in a solid return to the investors and employees, all of whom paid taxes on their income and returns.

(Side note: Jim is far from done in terms of contributing to the public good as he recently launched a new company! As the saying goes, "You can't keep a good man down.")

Less economically tangible, but far, far more important, is the contribution Jim has made to our family since his transplant: to our five children, our grandchild, our extended family, and to me. In addition to the daily moments of guiding and supporting us, Jim helped welcome our first grandson, Jackson, into the world. He was a significant part of our son Zachary's wedding, and helped shepherd the purchase and renovation of the newlyweds' first home. He watched our son, Christian, graduate from college, then helped him launch a fantastic career. He mentored our son, Joey, from a line role in his company to leading an office within his company. He has guided and supported our daughter, Brooklynne, in her development into a curious, car-enthusiastic, "let-me-try-and-fix-this," *Star Wars* and math-loving girl. No one else could have contributed to our family in the ways Jim has.

Had "the system" made the decision to put Jim on life support – keeping him alive – Jim would have been locked into mere existence. Yes, he would be alive, at least symptomatically, but he could not realize his full potential.

My eyes well up with tears as I consider this alternative as it relates to our family, and as I consider what our current policies do to hundreds of thousands of homeless and their families. We have put the homeless on "life support" under *Housing First* and *Harm Reduction*, versus giving them a chance to recover and fully contribute to their lives, their families, and the lives of others around them.

Yes, the short-term costs associated with deeper intervention can be higher – a $2 million transplant in Jim's case – but in the long run, the generational and societal costs to putting people on "life support" are far, far greater.

With all of my being, I know we can turn this crisis around. Whether you believe in evolution or creation, human beings are made to evolve within their own lifetimes – intellectually, emotionally, and spiritually. The homeless are no exception.

We will never completely end homelessness. There will always be new people entering into homelessness based on the deeper, ongoing issues highlighted throughout this book. We can end homelessness for the vast majority of individuals who experience it. But whenever you hear a policymaker say or promise to "end homelessness," please...run as fast as you can in the opposite direction.

Tackling this epidemic will not be easy. It will not happen overnight. It will require an "all-hands-on-deck" approach on the part of everyone – from the policy makers, to the voters, to the taxpayers, to the homeless.

The first step in "eating the elephant?" — Demand that our elected leaders engage in the very difficult but crucial policy discussions outlined in Chapter 16 – *Lessons to be Learned.* Demand they make policy decisions, and once they have made those decisions, hold them fully accountable to the outcomes promised.

This is a vast departure from what is happening today!

At the federal level, I suggest the President and Congress execute the following changes immediately. I say "immediately" because, as we witnessed under the initial *Housing First* roll out, it takes years for federal policy to trickle down to the local levels of government that hold the reins of responsibility for health and human services delivery. We need to take immediate action to prevent the "Homelessness Tsunami" just beyond our shores.

1. Require HUD to reassess its definition of a "homeless family" to align with the Federal Department of Education's, to provide a solid baseline on the numbers of homeless in the United States. This will force HUD and the nearly 350 other government entities that have adopted *Housing First*

to no longer ignore the rapidly increasing numbers of homeless women and children in America.

2. Change homelessness policy to allow for the creation and funding of a homelessness continuum that supports individual growth and progression. It must include multiple entry points and an ability to support the unique needs of people who enter homelessness. Additionally, it must include an understanding that growth will vary from person to person and must require the tracking of both short-term and long-term outcomes, including recidivism. Finally, government must adequately fund the development and administration of the tracking system.

3. Demand that the appropriate body of the Federal Government evaluate the research HUD employs in their claim that *Housing First* is "evidence-based" for all struggling with homelessness. Conduct further research to examine long-term outcomes of *Housing First* across all segments of the homeless population, and the true recidivism rates per segment.

Request that the same body evaluate the research used to support the *Harm Reduction* policy. Conduct further research, including an analysis of the long-term outcomes from *Harm Reduction* interventions. Currently, there is little to no long-term research looking at the impacts among the addicted sub-populations, including the homeless population.

Use both short and long-term data to analyze, evaluate, and determine where, if, and how *Housing*

First and Harm Reduction play a role in the new continuum.

4. Designate the federal Administration for Children and Families within the U.S. Department of Health and Human Services – rather than HUD – as the agency responsible for homeless families. This will maximize both effectiveness and the limited funding available to serve families.

5. Abolish the *Continuum of Care Boards* (CoCs), an oppressive web of bureaucracy created under *Housing First.* CoCs are yet another layer of bureaucracy that further dilutes available funding as well as accountability.

What's more, many of the board members of each local CoCs also receive its funding. The conflicts of interest the COCs present, in addition to the inherent resistance to change they promote, create dysfunction and significant potential for fraud.

Imagine the Department of Defense distributing a "Request for Proposal" for a sophisticated new spacecraft, then leaving the decision to a board of the very contractors submitting bids. Unable to choose between themselves, they begin working behind the scenes to ensure each contractor/board member benefits from "a piece of the action." Even if the most ethical individuals sit at that table, the situation is rife with the potential for corruption.

6. Create new partnerships with the private sector, churches, and philanthropic organizations to align

support for the entities within the new growth-focused continuum.

7. Encourage state and local governments to follow suit. As shared earlier, 350 government entities followed HUD into the *Housing First* trenches. Getting them to change course, again – to completely retool their systems from doing permanent housing only – to a system that will require much more effort will prove no easy task.

8. Encourage private sector involvement in the development of models and tracking systems. Replicate what works based on data: Better ideas, better testing, better data, and – most importantly – better results.

"If you think you are too small to make a difference, you've never been in bed with a mosquito."

AFRICAN PROVERB

Every Effort Counts

With government spending tens of billions of dollars on homelessness, individual donations – even those from foundations, corporations, churches, and service organizations – may seem small by comparison. **Not the**

case. These entities have launched many organizations such as Saint John's, and they continue to make a huge difference today. Indeed, the unsung heroes we shared in Chapter 17 are alive today due to donations from these entities.

What's more, they often provide volunteers to further assist these non-profits. If you, the reader, fall into one of these categories, please know your investment is extremely meaningful.

Today we ask you to extend your investment to the ballot box, to demand that elected leaders, both at the federal and local levels, adopt growth-focused homelessness policies. Demand they report back on a formal, quarterly basis through a framework of key metrics, including: number of persons in the continuum, number of persons in each category within the continuum, number of persons that exited the continuum, and the actual costs per person.

The cost figures provide a crucial data point that the public should not overlook. Far too many elected officials neither ask for, nor understand, the real costs behind their homelessness interventions. Case in point: Sacramento County's monthly report from staff at one point boasted the placement of over 200 homeless persons into permanent housing. This sounds positive on its surface – …but the county continues to withhold cost information, despite multiple requests from one Supervisor to report on the associated expenses.

A supervisor on this project did his own back-of-the-envelope math to calculate that the county spent roughly $12 million to permanently house them for one year. Officials must consider the clear benefits of housing 250 individuals only in the context of spending $50,000 to house each individual for a single year.

Of important note: *The $12 million figure grossly understates the real costs. It does not include any of the ongoing costs of providing the lifelong housing subsidy, nor does it include the costs of the government subsidies used to develop the affordable housing in which the homeless are placed. Finally, it excludes costs that were likely incurred by other departments within the county system, such as health care services, transportation vouchers, and/or school lunch programs.*

Government officials will vehemently resist this kind of transparency, but we must insist on it!

"A lack of transparency results in distrust and a deep sense of insecurity."

DALAI LAMA

Rise and be Heard

In the story of *Erin Brockovich,* for example, one woman finally stands up to a massive foe – literally on a table – sick and tired of how she and others were made sick by the very people who had been paid to protect them (in her case, an unscrupulous insurance provider and corrupt government officials).

One person took the first step to tackle a problem that seemed to be so huge – a problem that was killing people, and that nearly destroyed an entire community. A simple analogy perhaps, but it serves us well. The time for you to stand on top of our table was yesterday. Now it's actually time to flip that table completely upside down.

How can one person even begin to make a dent in a big, nameless, government machine? How can we all be as transformative as Erin Brockovich?

1. Donate to, AND volunteer for, programs that provide growth-focused communities. The primary reason *Saint John's* survived the financial blow dealt by the County – with six weeks of notice – was that individuals, corporations, and foundations stepped in to stop the bleeding, allowing us room to breathe, retool, and formulate a new survival plan. Our Unsung Heroes experienced the same fallout. Donations, down to every copper penny, matter!

   Volunteering is equally as crucial. More than 300 volunteers cross over the *Saint John's* threshold each month. They help with meal provision, child care, office support, and many other roles. Moreover, by simply showing up, these volunteers make a very important statement to the clients – that they matter!

2. Provide funding to these programs to track growth-focused outcomes. Not only are the current tracking systems limited to the sole metric of permanent housing, but government contracts typically limit administrative funding – the umbrella under which the tracking of data is housed – to 10% of the total contract value, a woefully inadequate percentage for nearly every non-profit. Depending on the initiative, *Saint John's'* administrative costs ranged between 15-25%.

Yes, government should provide this funding, and hopefully, our combined advocacy efforts will result in them doing so. However, we will need to use private funding to build and fuel the initial stages of this tracking while government transitions to absorbing the full costs. Simply let the non-profit know that you'd like your donation to be used towards these efforts.

If we implement the changes outlined in this book, and work in concert to ensure these principles are followed at every level of government and society, we will see a dramatic reduction in homeless numbers and, at the same time, a huge surge in societal productivity.

I thank God every day for the incredible honor and privilege to serve at *Saint John's* – to work alongside thousands of women and their children. For thirteen years, I witnessed their transformation and had the opportunity to encourage and support them in becoming all they wanted to be. My social media hashtag (ever since hashtags became "a thing") was #bestjobintheworld.

Today, eighteen months after stepping down as CEO, one of my favorite daily activities is to receive calls and/or social media messages from my "other daughters." They reach out to update me on their activities, to seek advice, and for emotional support when needed. They know I have their best interest at heart, and that I will always be their second or third Mama – whether they like it or not. The love I have for them and for their children lays deeply inside me.

They continue to inspire me, to remind me about what's important, and to remember my calling. While it may sound pessimistic to say, I will never enjoy a more impactful or fulfilling role in my professional career – ever.

Just as I entered *Saint John's* – under God's plan and not my own – I stepped down from *Saint John's* as its CEO when my husband joined a company in Texas. It is the most difficult transition I have endured, but as I often reminded the *Saint John's* staff, "we are in the wrong business if we, ourselves, are unwilling to change."

We must be willing to change and to continue to grow. These values are core to life and core to lifting our country out of the homelessness epidemic.

From the bottom of my heart, I thank you for taking the time to read this book, to learn more about how this crisis emerged, and how together, we can emerge from it.

I hope you will join forces with me to ask the right questions and "place the ladder against the right wall," to ensure that every person who experiences homelessness is able to enter a growth-focused continuum and ultimately exit to a better place, as a better person.

"You can choose to not be a warrior. But you cannot choose to 'not' be in the war."

UNKNOWN

CHAPTER 19

Closing the Gap

The individuals struggling with homelessness, addiction, mental illness, and/or domestic violence, did not grow up saying, "Boy, I am so excited to live in a tent along the river someday! I just can't wait to become so addicted to drugs that I lose my mind – or to become a criminal with an endless rap sheet that lands me in prison!"

On the contrary, the majority want to do better in life, and to live a meaningful, purposeful existence. They have lost their way, but with the proper support, they can realize real and lasting change.

When our neighbor suffers, we suffer, too. When they stumble and fall, we fall with them. Providing them the help they need, however, is not a job for government alone. It is not a job for our churches alone. Nor is it a burden for non-profit organizations to shoulder alone. As a community, as a country, we must do this together.

On behalf of Sheila, Adrianna, Alicia, Mandy, Jennifer, Natisha, Olliver, Julianna, Michelle and Alexandria and their families, on behalf of all who are struggling with homelessness, thank you for stepping into the fire.

Sheila Revisited

Covered in bramble and overgrown weeds, now *shredded by the onslaught of several harsh winters, the remains of an old battered tent sit forgotten along the banks of the American River.*

Sheila no longer lives there.

Sheila moved on.

Once and for all, Sheila finally decided to change. One crumpled brochure and a simple phone call – if she had any idea of the new road it would lead her down.

Once her sole means of protection, it had now been eighteen months since she walked away from that old tent. And now, like a bad dream, that cruel world along the freezing river had become a distant and fading memory. With her very last ounce of strength, she had somehow found the courage to go and knock on that strange Red Door.

Her eyes had a bright new light pouring out from them as she walked out that same door, now a different person than when she had walked through it the first time. She felt clear and strong now. Sobriety felt good, too.

Sheila looked back at the Red Door *and the women, all standing there, smiling at her, waving. She looked down at the new professional resume she held in her hands. She didn't know it at this emotional moment, but everything she had worked through over the last year and a half was about to blossom into a new job as well. In the midst of her farewell, she had no way of knowing she would soon become a celebrity employee at a local coffee house, loved and appreciated by all those who would work with her. How could she have imagined such a foreign concept? But as tightly as she gripped her new resume, she held onto even tighter to a new sense of hope.*

Returning the smile and waving back to her incredible new family, tears welled up in her eyes. She would miss them all so much. These people had genuinely loved her. They had taught her so much. They had saved her. Her thoughts drifted to that scroungy little mutt, J.J. He didn't have to die the way he did. So much sorrow. So much pain. But all of that was in the past now. All sins forgiven.

She inhaled deeply, then turned. With a new sense of strength, courage, and commitment, Sheila took the next step into a new life.

And the world will be
better for this
That one man, scorned
and covered with scars,
Still strove with his last
ounce of courage
To reach the unreachable,
the unreachable,
The unreachable star

Closing Thoughts

No doubt, this book will be perceived as controversial, perhaps inflammatory, especially by many policy makers and their staffs, who wholeheartedly adopted *Housing First* as their one-size-fits-all solution to homelessness. How do I know this, and why do I use the words controversial and inflammatory?

As *Saint John's* CEO, one of my primary responsibilities was advocacy. As I began to understand the underpinnings of *Housing First* – that it views every individual through the same lens and ignores the underlying issues that lead people to homelessness – and as I saw the public policy tide quickly shifting in this direction, I shared my concerns with policy makers and their staff.

I knew about the risks of this approach as it relates to children who have experienced significant trauma, and to women struggling with addiction and other trauma-related issues as well. I did not criticize *Housing First* as "an" approach, rather on "the" approach.

They defended their positions vigorously. I quickly earned pariah-like status with them, and other non-profits that wanted to remain in Goliath's good graces.

Our discussions focused on best practices in substance-abuse disorder treatment and trauma-informed care, and on *Saint John's'* over 30 years of experience in working with this population. Now, in 2020, we finally have data – comprehensive and compelling federal data – illustrating its failures as "the" solution to homelessness.

The decision is, of course, yours, but it cannot be put off – sitting on the fence will only get you splinters. Sweeping change and sweeping action are needed immediately to ensure that today's homeless crisis does not become a tomorrow's disastrous tsunami.

Affordable Housing

Some readers may wonder why I don't talk more about the issue of affordable housing. While the majority of today's homeless might eventually need affordable housing, right now they need temporary housing, along with services to address their underlying issues.

Even if you believe that an "affordable housing unit" is the "end-all-be-all" solution to homelessness, in the states where a lack of affordable housing has become a significant issue, lawmakers will not address the factors that have led to a virtual halt on its production. Case in point: billions of dollars in affordable housing bonds sit untapped in California today.

The stark truth is that "building more affordable housing" has become an all too convenient veil behind which too many elected officials hide. Very few propose anything else for the homeless while refusing to compromise on the regulatory barriers to building more affordable housing. We can no longer wait on them to pierce the veil. It is up to "We the People."

You, like me, might wonder how *Saint John's'* outcomes compare to those of a *Housing First* provider. It's a relevant question but unfortunately, one that we cannot fully answer. Based on the plentiful data *Saint John's* collects, in contrast to the one metric *Housing First* providers collect, we cannot conduct an "apples to apples" comparison. In a perfect world, we would hire a research university, at a pretty hefty price tag, to conduct a five-year longitudinal study providing such a comparison.

A Word About Religion

Based on the organization's name itself, I have been asked a million times if *Saint John's* is a religious or spiritual organization. The better question, I think, especially in the context of high barrier requirements, is whether or not a certain religious viewpoint or doctrine is promoted or even mandated.

Given the name *Saint John's*, and given the organization's roots on the steps of *St. John's Lutheran Church*, it is an understandable question. While *Saint John's* is not a religious organization, faith in God has absolutely played a major role in the success stories profiled, as well as hundreds of other *Saint John's* alumnae. We never mandate a commitment to pursue spiritual growth, but it is readily available for those who desire it. With success and growth as the prime objective, to ignore that inner aspect of a woman seeking to turn her life around would seem negligent.

Faith, as each person defines it, is what I consider to be the "third leg on the stool" of real change. As explained earlier, *Saint John's* helps women to heal physically, emotionally, and mentally. It partners with churches such as *Bayside* and *St. John's Lutheran* to provide each woman the opportunity to build a spiritual foundation that will ensure her success.

Similar to how we regard *Alcoholics Anonymous* and *Narcotics Anonymous* for an addict, we encourage a woman to attend both the addiction recovery groups offered at *Saint John's,* while also connecting them with outside groups. Staying connected with these groups will make her much more likely to remain on the path of sobriety. The same concept applies toward her spiritual development. If she is connected with a church both inside and outside of our walls, she is much more likely to have the support she needs to stay on the path.

A Lasting Memory

In closing, I am dedicating this book to the memory of three beautiful people – all *Saint John's* alumnae – who are unfortunately no longer with us:

Candice (2011), Barbara (2020), and Miss Frankie (2020), also a long-time, beloved employee. Their lives were cut way too short and far too soon. But during their time with *Saint John's*, each made meaningful contributions to their families and fellow alumnae, living out the maxim that "While ripping off the Band-Aid is not fun – it must be done."

These amazing women informed *Saint John's*. They each informed me. And they each informed this book.

Special Thanks

I thank God for the opportunity to have served at *Saint John's*, including meeting and serving thousands of women and children. As it was for them, my inner light was sparked while there. And like them, I have "graduated," as His plan for me continues.

I thank my family for "sharing me" for thirteen years. I now see much more clearly the sacrifices they made – definitely taking the short end of the stick in the deal, and rarely complaining about it – at least not to me directly ☺. I am extremely grateful to them for both their sacrifices and their tremendous help along the way. They have volunteered, donated, recruited, taught…and so much more.

Thank you to my partners in this endeavor – David Flanagan and Julie Smithey. This book took us the better part of a year to complete, and not only were they there every step of the way, but they made the process fun… well, as fun as writing a book could possibly be ☺. It would have never materialized without these two soldiers. I am deeply touched by their friendship and their commitment to getting the story right. I am also deeply grateful to, and for, Kayla Wood, who edited the book during the unexpected challenges of overseeing Zoom lessons for her three children.

Thank you to the women who shared their stories – women who represent the thousands of women and children who have walked through the *Red Door* and whose lives are forever changed because of it. Sheila,

Sherri, Olliver, Adrianna, Alicia, Jennifer, Julianna, Natisha, Alexandria and Michelle – each now serve as examples in my life, in the lives of their children and family members, in the lives of their fellow sisters, and now, hopefully, in your life as well.

Thank you to our "along the way" readers who helped us shape this book to ensure our story was most effectively told: Jim Jeffers, John Mejia, Amy and Ted Gay, Colleen Wilcox, Owen Brown, Irene Sabourin, Lance Izumi, Lexi Robertson, Dawn Davison, Holly Parrish-Bezner, Zach Steeb, Jim Steeb, Susie Patterson, Blake Lentz, and Annie Robertson.

Thank you to those individuals who have endorsed this book and the need for this story to be told: The Honorable Chuck Devore, The Honorable Don Nottoli, The Honorable Angelique Ashby, Pastor Frank Espegren, Pastor Bob Balian, Jeff Henderson, Bill Whalen, Dawn Davison, and Christopher Rufo.

Thank you to the *Saint John's* staff, past and present, who have been a part of building the organization and who continue to fuel the mission. In my thirteen years of working there, it would be nearly impossible to list them all, but each deserves my gratitude for their magnificent commitment. In particular, I would like to thank Wanda Jackson, Donna Russell, Maureen Gagliardi, Abra Ruthenbeck, Susan Barron, Nicole Brock, Heidi Stauffer, and Sasha Wirth, each of whom helped to shape *Saint John's* in deeply meaningful ways.

Thank you to *Saint John's* Board members, past and present, who have shared and continue to share their time, treasure, and talents to ensure *Saint John's* success. In particular, Kathy McKim and Chet Hewitt, both of whom served for many years as Board Chair and both of whom shared their wisdom and encouragement that got us through some incredibly trying times. I'd also like to thank David Flanagan once more, my co-author, who led and underwrote the re-branding of *Saint John's* and who continues to shepherd it at the Board level today. Finally, I'd like to thank Kevin Ramos and Buzz Oates for spearheading the *Saint John's* campus project and for their continued commitment.

Thank you to the many non-board-member advisors who counseled me and *Saint John's* in very impactful ways – in particular, Denny Samuel, Russell Austin, and Chuck Longanecker.

Thank you to all of the *Saint John's* donors and volunteers who bolster the effort day in and day out – in particular *St. John's Lutheran Church* (our birth parent, the reason behind *Plates Midtown,* and a significant supporter overall), Bayside Church (a significant source of volunteers, financial support, and the provider of onsite church services), Bob Murphy, Gary Johnson and Pete Kolak for the donation of countless hours to help disseminate our message, and to Bobbin and Patrick Mulvaney who helped formulate and launch our first social enterprise, *Plates Café and Catering*, and so much more.

Thank you to Mike Duffy and to Jim Roque, both of whom I met along the way and who served as models in the "jumping hurdles" – what it takes to overcome them, and how to apply the principles I've learned beyond women and children.

Last but not least, I would like to thank the City of Sacramento for stepping forward to fill in where the County of Sacramento has clearly fallen down in addressing the homelessness crisis, including the funding of *Saint John's*. Not only does the City understand there is no one-size-fits-all solution to homelessness, they put their money where their mouth is by recognizing, and providing funding for, different approaches for addressing homelessness.

"If nothing ever changed, there would be no butterflies."

ANONYMOUS

About the Authors

MICHELE STEEB

With over 13 years of on-the-ground experience working directly in homelessness, Michele transformed *Saint John's Shelter*, a simple 30-day homeless pitstop, into an effective, comprehensive 18-month program serving over 270 women and children each day, helping and guiding them in actively addressing and overcoming the root causes of their poverty and homelessness. As a result, *Saint John's Program for Real Change* has become the largest program of its kind in the State of California.

In addition, during her tenure, she launched three additional entrepreneurial enterprises within the organization: *Plates Café and Catering, First Steps Child Development Center*, and *Plates Midtown*, all of which serve as hands-on "real world" employment training for the homeless. She grew *Saint John's* initial $1 million annual operating budget (originally over 75% reliant on government funding) to a substantial $7.5 million budget with a significantly diversified funding base, including earned income from social enterprises, multiple public funding sources, and a stronger base of individual, foundation, and corporate support. In addition, Michele orchestrated a 5-year, $1.8 million contract with the State of California to do the same for women transitioning from prison.

MicheleSteeb.com
michelesteeb@gmail.com

DAVID M. FLANAGAN

An active Board Member with *Saint John's*, David has worked closely with Michele over the last seven years, gaining a deeper understanding of the problems that cause homelessness and the solutions that provide real and lasting results. Founder of a celebrated California brand agency, *Misfit,* he is the author of three books, including his international bestseller, *Rudder-Strategic Brand Clarity*.

FlanaganSpeaks.com
dflanaganbz@gmail.com